The Book of Her

by Shake The Poet

I0150329

From The Richard White Collection

Copyright © 2019 by Richard White All rights reserved.
This book or any portion thereof may not be reproduced or used in any manner whatsoever without the expressed written permission of the author except for the use of brief quotations in a book review. The views and opinions expressed in this book do not necessarily represent that of 310 Brown Street, its owner or employees.

Released July 2019

Printed in the United States of America
Published by 310 Brown Street
Edited by Sunni Soper & Christopher Michael
Cover Design by D. Brown
ISBN 978-0-9998291-8-9
Published by 310 Brown Street
www.310brownstreet.com
310brownstreet@gmail.com
shakethepoet@gmail.com
www.shakemadness.com

I was there for you, cared for you
Fought your fears and was scared for you
How dare you leave me out here bare and unaware
For you…. I worked around the clock, nonstop
I got stabbed and shot, in shock
Yeah, you were there when I got stitched up…
Yet when I needed you there most, you bitched up
I didn't earn a spot on this team just to get cut once I was picked up…
You used to use me didn't you
Kept me smitten, I kept forgiving you
I should've gotten rid of you when I was the subject of your ridicule
But I didn't, didn't you notice who stood closest
When you were goal-focused, did you notice, did you note this
Did you write this in your diary, next to where you'd lie to me
About what you'd confide in me, friend you did pretend but
Never really tried to be, you cried to me
I was ready to give my life and die…for me……you'd avert your eyes
Cold shoulder, you weren't the soldier you were supposed to be
Thought we were closer – a poser, I was sold a dream
I was sold alive, I was sold a lie
You rescinded, had it amended, would have me 'Amen' it
I used to hang suspended, publicly displayed, you're fickle
Ain't much has changed, since them days I slaved and wasn't paid a nickel
Since I've been able, you've been Kane, plain and simple
You've made my pain a symbol, now our children view our history through a tainted window
I wouldn't have built your roads if I would've known you wouldn't take me with you
Maybe that's why I was forced, I didn't speak the language
You're a liar, whitewash
I was a fool to believe, I've been fooled and deceived
To bleed for your greed for green, tricks up your sleeve
I've made the pavement crack, I've laid the tracks
In return you gave me scraps, you gave me crack
You'd say we "blacks don't know how to act," so you laid the strap to my back
Clap, when I'm entertaining you
I'm just a slave to you
Ain't it true…
Convinced me to board your ships, hoping to be led down the right paths
Instead you left my blood, my blues painted on your white flags
Your system… convinced me to vaccinate my children
With your chemicals designed to assassinate my children
I've been getting fucked, while your Master baits my children into your prisons

7

Or to be delivered to those that assassinate my children
You've been burying my seeds, uprooting my trees and burning my leaves
Now you're choking, smoking my weed, but I'm in the joint
100 Proof, but I'm behind the bar, a life so tender
Guilty 'Till' proven innocent, Emmitt ain't the end of it
The Angel of Death and I have gotten intimate, visits me often, closed coffins
Walking home – to simply never arrive
Why my daughter can't go into police custody and come out alive
You're always killing something
I thought we were friends, thought we were building something
One nation under a façade and misrepresentations of God
You got me – Oh you got me good, maybe I misunderstood
I thought I heard, "Repair Nations" instead of "Reaper's Waiting"
Never asked for reparations, why you got your weapons aiming
I thought we were friends
You murdered my parents before you took me in
Now I've grown homesick for a place I've never been
I thought that after all this time there'd be some improvement
But I've been enduring the abuse for your amusement
You like halting my movements, poisoning my music and playing me for stupid
Stupid me, for thinking you could turn a slave-ship into a friendship…
A non-existent friendship can never be kinship
Stupid me for thinking different
Broken hearted as if we parted ways….
We ain't ever have them days
Then it hit me….
Shame, I had to see 50 something stars
Before I could just accept who you really are
My enemy

Permission to speak candidly....
Since the new theme of the American dream...
Is to identify with, whatever the fuck you want to identify with
Can I no longer identify with.... Black
It's just a hue man,
But I ain't been hu-man
Since you've labeled me, it's just one of the names you gave to me to
describe the greatness that came with me...
There's something I possess that you lack
There's something my veins pack that you tried to scrape from my back
Chains, weights on my back
Whips cracked, spit at, cause I was black
Back of the bus, colored section, sectioned off opportunity when you got
through with me in servitude
Oh, but you loved me when I was serving you....
So much that you gave me the Good Book and His Only Begotten to look
up to....
Fuck You
Know that I am God
I am not black, I am not void, I cannot be destroyed
Don't call me black, black means target, battle hardened
Black means, threat, that boy can catch, look at him run
Black means, he got a gun, he's stealing, check his pockets
Black means, do you have any sharp objects
Black means, no progress....
Black means, you're a silhouette, they just ain't kill you yet
Black means, Officer pull the trigger, you may as well call me a nigga
I'm the same God, you've lied about in your exaggerations in the scriptures
The same blood sacrifice gave to the Natives from the Pilgrims
The same God the Pillagers spoke of to the Villagers before they pillaged
them, started killing them
Black means, wretched, woeful, disastrous
I am not Sin in Name
Black means, sullen, dismal, wicked, evil
I've never slaughtered or enslaved a People
I've never allowed a feeble ego to make me treat other people unequal
My skin natural brown, cocoa plant, vanilla bean, mahogany
I am gold, bronze and ebony, I am heavenly
To you, black means trouble, black means devil
Black means, lower level, like the bowels of slave ships
Black was the whip they whipped the slaves with
To you black ain't shit
I've never blacklisted blackness, black is without vision
Though you never mention that black is without limits

While white is without life or living, white is blinding
White means pale, pale means weak, weak means pathetic
Pathetic means inadequate, inadequate means spiritless
Spiritless means spineless, lifeless, cowardice
Black don't know what power is, to you black is powerless
I identify with the 'Most High,' keep my head high
You say, "In God we trust," I won't let me down
Come hell or high water, know I *(Noah)* won't let me drown
God is eternal, blackness is everlasting, everlasting means eternal
To be God means to be Black, but don't call me that
I don't identify with your lies, guise or descriptions
You can't temper my pigment
You've been selling melanin for a profit, I am Moor than a Prophet
Moorish, Coptic…. Born with this chocolate, this onyx
You want to disable and murder me
Because my skin sable and burgundy
Black means, punished for something they didn't do yet for being brunette
Black means atrocious, hopeless
Black is what smoke is
White is what dope is, white is what coke is
There's a truth you choose not to reveal, white means to kill
To you, black means conflicted, afflicted
To me, white means addiction
You won't make the correlation, white means to abhor a nation
To me, black means Guyanese, Lebanese, Senegalese
To you, black means nigga please
Hoping that weed choking them nigga seeds
Uprooted, branched out, hoping that nigga leaves
Black means bodies hanging from nigga trees
Black means nigger, bigger, faster
Black means in need of Master, make kneel to master
Black means sweating in the pastures, the fields
Black means forced to yield, black means abort and kill
Black means not worth it, God means I'm perfect
Black means the killing of children that aren't birthed yet
Black means forgotten, but we haven't forgotten
Black means rotten
Black means Monkey, will play for money
My bronze means experimented on
Lab Rats aren't black
Black means killed when read, writing, Blues, hushed
Black means dread, the Whites and Ku Klux
God means Sun will rise, rise means to climb, rise means to survive
Black means unalive, white means undead
Black means spirit-filled even when spirit-killed by bloodshed
Black means forbidden, black means stolen
Black means to be chosen, chosen is to be God

God is to be black, black is to be God
White is to lack, Whites against Blacks, means to lack God
Call me Niger, Angola, Buffalo Soldier
Zimbabwe, Zaire, Black means nappy hair
Black means resilient, Black means strong
God means power, God means all
Black means knock me down, I won't fall
You don't deserve to call me black, don't call me that
Call me God
When you speak my name, recall the chains
When you speak my name, recall the hanging
When you say my name, recall the pain
When you say my name recall the slave
Recall the black bodies lying lifeless
Say my name, Horus, Ra, Anubis, Osiris
I've suffered, but I've not suffered an identity crisis, survived genocide
Know who I am, I ask not to be indemnified
I just demand to be identified.... As who the fuck I am
I demand you understand, I'm a man
I demand you understand that I am Black....

And God.........damn

~She asked,
"What goes on in a mind as alone as mine"
I replied…. ~

I've never kept the windows clean
There were things, I figured best left unseen
Living a dream, ain't always what it seems
I wouldn't let them see – the skeletons in my closet
Chase me into the bathroom, I used to vomit
Nights I went up in a rocket and was brought down by a comet
Nightmares, awaiting me at the top of my stairs
Memory lapses – but I never forget them, I get them often
Four walls of a coffin, I get lost in thought
There'd just be more stuff to burn once it's furnished
Loud banging of the furnace
I have more shit to be concerned with
Like this earnest purpose I'm concerned with
I'm concerned with – keeping my dirty laundry in the hamper, stains out of my carpet
But every time folks throw rocks, my house seems to be the target
They aim at what they think they see, but the blind don't know
They speculate and suppose because my blinds are closed
In this house....
I've been repainting the walls with my tears for years
From every nook and cranny, every indentation and depression filled with depression
A Gun Case of weapons, that I choose not to use
Afraid if I cock one, I know not which side I'd choose
Which lives I'd lose, suicide or home- inside I'm bruised
Paintings of ghosts on the walls, see my smile hanging there
Lights off, cause my tribulations and trials tend to glare
I sit and stare in to space, just taking up space, I'm a waste, I'm a mess
Stressed up to my waist, pain up to my neck
I don't expect strangers to understand, these are my secrets
I discuss my deepest with the demons I sleep with
I've just been sleepless, so every weakness has been leaked
In this house....
The floor boards creak, nobody walking
I've heard voices in my head, but nobody talking
Beneath the rustling of the grass, snake's slither, dog's barking
In this hell, imprisoned, no don't tell I vision
Because the News is always just my story being told by people who've never peeked in my peephole
Something in the attic is pure evil
Yet the cellar dwellers and hellions are housed in my bowels
There's so much shit in my pits that I put up with
That I'm up with the Vampires and bloodsuckers hanging from the ceilings
Kept the best company with my feelings, a man died in this house

13

And his soul just wants out
In this house....
The walls are padded, nut cased, straight jacket
Because self-mutilation only stops when restraints happen
Tubs filled, radio silenced
I've had thoughts of trying it
Been prying these desires of dying from inside of me
When nobody is beside me
I've been beside myself for so long, we've decided to get to know one
another...
We have nothing in common, but we have an understanding
In this house, there's the same picture in every mirror
I look into and ask, ... "Who is that man in it?"
I wonder... if I'd open these doors, if they can see the vacancies....
In this house
Imagine that I could possibly escape with ease, but I'm too afraid to break the
lease....
In this house

Have you ever experienced a relationship...
That felt like you were with a bitter Ex
And the only time you could come together was during sex
Stress ripped you apart – the bitter with the sweet
Conversations no longer deep, weak foundation
Trapped in a box, both different views, staring at separate walls across the room
Back to back you can't sleep
You can't speak with civility; the ability escapes you
Loving someone who hates you, has a tendency to break you
It makes you unhappy, unrecognizable and unhinged
At the very thought of another confrontation you clasp and cringe
What happened to the 'Friend,' you used to be before you got used to me
What happened to the 'Them,' we used to be, when beautifully we'd blossom
I can't even be the 'Me,' I used to be, cause you don't see a need for me
Mistreating me emotionally, noticeably we aren't as close as we're supposed to be
Fronting for the world socially, but we can never express ourselves openly
What man is attracted to a woman detached from her femininity, sensitivity
What woman wants a man who hasn't a backbone to stand
So eager to please, yet so easily beaten to his knees
Why keep beating him???
You've been keeping them, but can't even remember what it is you used to see in them
Have you ever felt alone in their presence, suffering from depression
Ever have them hug you physically and feel no intimacy only pressure
Did you stop feeling like treasure, when they began kicking you with the rocks
Did it make you hold on a bit tighter, thinking that this was all that you've got
Crazy – when the tempers got hot and you can't stop throwing shots
Have you sat back and watched your relationship leave the docks...
Viewing the burning and crashing, wearing different masks
Pretending to be passionate, trying to capture a moment
Holding on to memories, while 'meant to be's' grew empty
What used to be good and plenty, simply ain't enough
When the going gets tough, it seems like they've kept their bags packed with their baggage
When their soft and sweet became savage
It's just not right-
For a man to find a wife, to be the loneliest you've been in your life
You ever felt deaf, dumb and mute cause you had no one to talk to
No one to understand
What says a woman to her man who always wants the upper hand
What says a man to his wife, who thinks she'd be better off without him
They can't see the cultivation made them better than when you found them
Choking back more than enough tears than it'd take to drown them
Did you love them but couldn't stand to be around them
Did you surround them with love, but they kept finding an escape

Did you get lost finding yourself asking "how much more can I take"
The weight of your burden is hurting and you're uncertain of the stability
Tip toeing emotions – out of your mind only focusing on agility
Cause you know you ain't tripping…. You know you ain't tripping
Something's missing and you're giving it your all
You just want someone who'll answer when you call
That'll carry you when you fall, winter, summer, spring and all
Instead of finding reasons to change every season
She used to make breathing easy for a man who had been dying trying
He once made her happy, but through the smiling he can tell that she's lying
Iron sharpens iron, but it takes fire to mold it
Did you ever feel like things became obligations because they were owed it
Or had a hard time remembering the last moment that felt so good, you had to hold it
It just felt right……………………
Have you ever been in hell…
Cause that's exactly…what it feels like

Last night I laid in bed, eyes open
physically unable to close them
mentally unable to focus
hopelessness on the horizon
between I and Zion, but the Sun ain't ...rising
my insides crying
outside, tears hiding
and I ain't finding someone to confide in
too busy trying to abide by my Heart's rules
feeling I'm too good to make dark moves
until my Heart proves that Shark food ain't in its contents
I can't trust its contents, it's complex....
Feeling like my mind's next, I'm stressed
I feel it in my spine, neck
my eyes check, but see nothing in my reflection
simply disrespecting, the direction I was headed in
a missed connection and regretting are like sedatives setting in
But I can't swallow those pills, It'd kill me
like this pain is gonna heal me
since I can't feel the rain, it's the rain that fills me
hence my Cup runneth
my stomach plummets, punish myself cause my health suffers
try to think to myself but my lips utter
placing head under covers doesn't make morning come sooner
I reach out to the Father, let Him know I miss Junior
I'm like a Shark in the water, an Ape in the tree
Not quite King of this Jungle, but I'm destined to be
As a Dragon in the heavens, the only danger is me
smoke emits from my nostrils, fire from the lungs
realizing how many I've stung with the venom of this tongue
I'm a Lover, I'm a Fighter
I admire my desires and ambition
but I'm swinging and missing, hitting myself
my intentions are good, often misunderstood
don't always piece together these puzzles as fast as I should
I'm not perfect by a long shot
not willing to take the wrong shot just to see what I'm shooting
thoughts may Control-Alt-Delete, but the Heart keeps rebooting
too stupid and foolish, so clueless I remain
I'm in ruins and don't know what I'm doing in these chains
30-something hours since I've eaten a thing
can't wrap my mind around the meal without Fellowship of the Ring
therefore I'm empty when there is plenty enough to leave me filled
but I lay awake not counting sheep, but how many times I've been killed
I'd rather nest in my blessings

an essence so refreshing, no recollection of the lesser
but my lesser is becoming greater and my greater becoming lesser
somehow I missed that message
sleepless nights followed by days of stomach rumbles and stumbles
leaves a man vacant, a Vagrant who roams the streets and mumbles
try not to live homeless when home is where the heart is
tired of watching these dreams get shot down, seems mine are the target
Lost in the emptiness of this abyss, broken in half
trying to find my way home and how to be whole, when all I have
....is two halves.

Failure was never an option until my first attempt at suicide, but look at me now...
Breathing and shit
Born prematurely, respirators – wheezing and shit
Feeling like God had forsaken, wasn't believing in shit
Hardened by hunger and homelessness, why'd they leave me in shit
When you're the dependent of the chemically dependent, you stop depending on people
Affection becomes ineffective when more than the injections are lethal
Being abused by abusers who are abusing themselves
Gruesome tales, I knew them well
A choice between that freedom or imprisonment, I'd choose the cell
It wasn't until I failed at taking my life, that I knew I'd prevail
I was more worried about dying black, than dying in Iraq
More confused about how to tell my teachers that I was scratched by a cat, rather than attacked when I didn't own a cat
More afraid of the fact I knew, if ever I'd stopped smiling, I would snap
41 days I went to school with everything I owned on my back
I know what it's like to lack, back against the wall
Too strong to fall, back against the wall
Took two steps forward and still found myself back against the wall
Told myself to "Go hard or Go home," with no home to go to
My journey in life, didn't go like it was supposed to
Created shelters in my mind, to not let the winter's cold through
Fell to my knees many times and cried
Said to the voice in my head, "I heard you! Young Boy, Man up!"
I had to relearn to stand-up
My perseverance is admirable
Been suffering from Post-Traumatic Stress long before it was fashionable
Before I ever bled on the battlefield, my entire life was battle filled
I've had to teach myself 'I Can'
When times got hard, of course I believe in God, 'I am'
My face shows no trace of the scars I have
Like tar over scabs, I keep these demons sealed
Only minor pieces revealed
Too hard to conceal when I know how missed meals feel, unable to deal with the pressure
When the flames consume everything that you treasure, but you measure up
Know what it's like crying myself to sleep, petrified of my dreams
Back and forth with my thoughts, paranoid from the screams
Consumed by the dark rooms and chambers
The isolation fueling my anger made me fall in love with the danger
But I was frightened
The noose on my neck began to tighten before I began writing
Dying inside before I began fighting my silence

Couldn't find an escape until I decided to write it
Imagine a train of thought so vivid, you could ride it
I've sat and watched life pass by and never notice me
No 'Woe Is Me'
Potential was trapped with my innocence until I broke us free
Black skin, gold heart, I am all Art
Pain in my roots, soul and bark
Search for the beauty in life, I began to embark
Prisoner of my own oppression, slave to my thoughts, until I began to march
I was my biggest threat until I began to step, until I ran from stress
Became Man and Weapon
When they thought, I was just another nigga with a temper and skeletons
I learned to prove myself better than
I had to learn that they'll never understand....
That when coming from strife, when life is in your hands
Failure is not an option, it's a plan
And I had planned on taking; falling, never to awaken
Mistaking, I was breaking
It wasn't until I was facing the mirror, tasting my tears – wrist to razor that I gave up
Picked up Pen and Paper and wrote myself a savior
Been penciling pain in my poems, prophecy out of failures
Taking my last breaths
Praying my audience can inhale them
My soul I share cause I've lived long enough to tell them
Suicide is much like failure…. It doesn't end well.

The weak hold grudges
The strong hold position
So, if we never speak again….
Know that you've already been forgiven
Once cut from the same cloth
But these stitches need re-mending
Tried to suture our future looking for closure
Left a wound open to exposure, my guess is….
That you needed the attention
Hoping for facts to back your opinion
This turbulence and friction is all based on your fiction
We went to war… but we survived
The love died, but we're alive – at least I thought….
Cause I'm standing over your headstone reading your epitaph
Wishing, "Rest In Peace" to a lost soul
When I never made peace with the better half
No flowers or apologies
Let's not pretend that you were fond of me, or family
You abandoned me
But I'm left standing the way we'd planned to be
I can feel the cold wind blowing
I guess you're trying to answer me, chill…
I didn't come here to listen
I'm paying you this visit to cut up these pictures
And cut out these scriptures, images and visions
This is my first step to forgetting, getting into remission
I can bury with you, every whisper you mentioned
Every secret you muttered between the things you would utter
Life has a funny way of getting even
Watched you sell your soul to the devil to escape from your demons
Now you're no longer breathing, your light … no longer beaming
Dreaming of standing between you and the Reaper, my Brother's Keeper
Death is one hell of a teacher, cause I can still see ya but can't reach ya
Wasted opportunity between confusion and scrutiny
We'd become so dead to one another that your loss of life wasn't news to me
Beautifully laid bouquets can't rewind the days
To say what we forgot to say
Somethings never a rose from your two lips
I sat praying, hoping you would forget me not
You couldn't have been as heartless as I thought, for your heart to stop
I had both hands out, you ran out and so did your clock
I don't have time... to mourn, or be mad
Or to be saddened by the tragedy
Spent enough time battering back at me to get back at me

21

I had lost myself and had to get back to me gradually
Attacking me, myself – an eye for an eye
I couldn't see the reasons … you left my Mother, my Brother, both of my Sisters
Was it the heroin or the liquor
I thought Father Figure was a permanent fixture
If I were to list everything you've ever done for me on one hand
I couldn't give you the finger
I used to think you were mad at me
That you hated my Momma for having me
You were allowed to be proud
But you didn't stick around to see me hit the ground
And stand up running
To hit the track running
Streets of Iraq gunning
When I was stumbling, and tumbling, learning manhood from a woman
She was the wall and the cushion
When I felt that I couldn't, she told me to keep pushing
I stopped looking for a father
Cause you wouldn't bother to appear
I started to fear being a father, cause I thought fathers didn't care
What I look like being a father, having my mother help me to prepare…
I used to have every birthday card you sent me in a box of promises and memories
I threw them out for being empty
Never wanted sympathy, just the energy to let you go
I came to let you know…. That for once….
I thank you, for making time to talk to your son.

-That's how I define, 'Rest'…in this piece.

I've lost 15 friends in 18 months to suicide....
Smiled for the world, golden- but so blue inside
Falling apart at the seams, no glue inside, foolish pride
I dare not ask for help, how selfish
Who's there to pull you aside when no one is around
When those tears come down and drown your frown
Each day you wake up in clown make up
Trying to make up for time you've only lost in your mind
Would they mind, would they miss me, I've never felt so empty
So void – I just want to escape the noise
I'm still trying to hide from the pain, hiding my shame
I was told 'death is inevitable when you're riding the train'
And I'm trapped on these tracks, about to snap
Aim and shoot, blood stains on boots
Anti-depressants are depressing, pain killers are killing me
Sleeping pills haven't stopped me from awakening to this nightmare
I still fight for my life, though life won't fight fair
My daughter said, "Dad, why are you crying?"
And I started lying, how do I tell my child that I feel like I'm dying
That I'm only surviving through my writings
I'm man enough to admit that I'm scared
That I'm not as strong as I had imagined
That pain and passion has been clashing with Dragons
I've been outlasting the lashings by telling myself
That I'm not starving, I'm fasting, keep the seatbelt fastened when I'm crashing
When half of it, is being haunted by past tense, imagining being attacked by pacifists
You fear for the safety of those who're supposed to be safely in your care
Imagine looking past your children because you're too afraid to stare
Too afraid to bare any further burden
Hiding the hurting behind the curtains
My eyes disguise the lies of what lays inside so well
That sometimes even I believe that I'm well
No one to tell that I'm in hell, that I see a face, pale
That I can taste, smell – even hear my death at the door
That this is too familiar, that I've met him before
That death and my life became more acquainted each time I tried to take it
My Therapist said, "Get naked, be honest"
"Open up to people, not just the skeletons and monsters"
I thought that putting my mouth to the mic instead of a barrel
Would stop the unravelling... but I'm unravelling
It's baffling how hard I've been battling since I was battling in the battlefield
I thought the hard part was over
I guess this is what happens when you can't take the soldier out of a soldier....

I've lost 15 friends in 18 months to suicide…
And I'm ashamed to admit that I've tried to join them
I'm sure we've all cried out for help….
Apparently, we aren't the only ones who've just been hearing voices

Somethings…. Are better left unsaid
I can't sleep, yet most nights I wake up thinking I'd be better off dead
Imagine the feeling of being able to admit it without the fear of being committed
Fathom the regretting and depression, the lessons we take back
Imagine being turned into a weapon and you can't change back
Trauma has a way to pin men up in strange places
Images of brave faces who became faceless
Those who couldn't escape it, imagine losing every ounce of your sanity trying to replace it
I'm still searching for pieces to stitch back together….
I still talk to my friends who didn't make it
I still got friends who couldn't take it, so they took it themselves
This isn't the story we tell
These are my secrets protected
This ain't a war story, it's my Horror Flick, I'm just avoiding the credits
I'm survived by a Medic…. hell of a Soldier
She took that thing out of my shoulder, it was her first time giving sutures
And a whole platoon of shooters who left their minds in Fallujah, got me losing mine
Somethings…. Are better left unspoken
You get tired of bending when you're already broken
Knowing the gates of hell are open and these walls are closing in
I've lost a brother who locked himself in his home alone until they found his bones
And another who decided to run through traffic
Maybe I know magic
Cause I can see how the tragic happens, but I always manage to be subtracted from the equation
I keep escaping,
Unscathed, no visible scars
Trapped in this prison, no visible bars
I know help is out there, cause I've been out there with the help
But we were never trained to seek help for self
Never to shuffle the deck, just play the hand that we were dealt
If you can't muzzle the thought of your death, just keep it to yourself
You never learn to dig deep enough….
Laughter helps me hide my tears, been coping this way for years
Poetry is how I conceal carry my fears
I reminisce with Warriors whose memories are shot, no memory of being shot
A Soldier who kept his faith when he lost his face and ability to taste
We laugh about prosthetics, bolts, screws, pins and needles cause we need to
Forced to forge friendships because when strangers are around, it feels like I'm drowning
I don't really have a problem with crowds, I just don't like feeling surrounded
I started hugging to feel life – in the company of ghosts

Cause when being haunted by spirits, it feels good to touch the hosts
I've yet learned to calm my thoughts and focus
Just found a way to make sure no one noticed
I don't hear voices, this is screaming and screeching
Between the Angels that protect me and these demons
The chaos is peaceful, so I keep reaching
Somethings… are better left avoided
On the inside, I've died a few times and enjoyed it
All I did was sleep, no nightmares or bright flares of warfare
Nor the decaying flesh aroma, just an eternal coma after the battles were over
And soldiers were back with their families, no casualties
No depression or medication, no sedation or anger misplacing
No dangerous places invading my imagination
Instead I keep one fist clenched around this life I was willing to give
And the other cinched around my kids and rib, the reasons why I live
Somethings…. Are best openly and honestly expressed, and I just did….
I only look up, cause I have nothing left to give…

I just want to write….
If I had a pen, it would've saved my life
Give me a pen, and it could change my life
I got life in this pen, I should be writing again
I'm not fighting with them, I'm fighting within

I can tell she's fearing me by the way she stares at me
She said that in this Pen, a pen ain't a part of my therapy
She ain't right, writing was helping me, this is unhealthy, it's hell for me
Trapped in a cage
Shining their bright light,
recording with their mic
This room is not for interrogation
it's a stage
Let me bleed my rage on the page
Don't strap me to this bed and give me meds
Get out of my head, I want to be fed lead instead
Make it sharper, I won't make a knife or a spike
I just want to write
Peace of mind, peace at life
It'll be alright if I write, there will be peace all night
Life…. Sentence
Sentences, sentences, sonnets, sestinas, syllables
Prescriptions refillable, I don't want to swallow the sedatives
It gets repetitive feeling so negative

Graffiti on the padded walls of this room I'm locked in
I just want to write-out…when I'm boxed in
I'm surgical with a pen….
Remove this straight jacket and I can tattoo all over my skin
I don't want to dream, I don't want to scream
I want to eat through reams
I want to write about demons
Write about how my father used to abuse my mother and molest my brother
Blood stains on his covers
Covered his mouth when he would shout, "Ouch, you're hurting me"
He was hurting him
I want to write about what made me murder him
I wasn't suffering from insanity, I was protecting my family

Let me out of here
If I had a pen…..
Maybe the voices would stop, the noises would stop
You think I'm crazy, maybe your poisons should stop

You just want to sedate me, claim I'm angry
You must hate me, trying to break me, I can't break free
There's no escaping the scathing, I just want to write a statement
Let me write nightly to remind me of where my days went
Days spent staring at the void, the absence, I'm no addict
This is not addiction, I can write a vivid description
depicting the figments I imagine
The passion for adding words to the unheard to be read....

If I was crazy, you'd already be dead

I want to write about the monsters in my closet and under my bed
And how the only time I feel safe is when I come off of my meds
I need to write about the killer in the mirror that's coming after me before I
become his casualty
I need to write about the bruises and battering that's happening
My brain wasn't made to decay, Momma why'd you let them take me away,
you made me this way
I just want to write what I have to say
They say I threw fits, wrote hieroglyphs on my wrists
They said I was Schiz
Claimed that I have a disorder, I was just writing without borders
Deep thoughts, now I'm drowning without water
I'm being eaten from the inside out, I need to let it out

Pumping me with Perphenazine, Xanax, and Ritalin
When I could be cured with scribbling, writing
Gagged me at the mouth when you feared the biting
Am I that frightening
Give me a pen and it could change my life
I just want to write

If I had a pen....
It would've saved my life.

I've never died before....
I don't know if it hurts
I don't know if it's worse than this curse I'm immersed in
I'm no longer the person I was, my first version
At birth I didn't know hurt or pain
I trained until I strained, and it began to drain me
It changed me, and now I'm so angry
I've tried to hang me, drug me, anything to unplug me
I had become so ugly, I couldn't love me
Didn't want me to continue
To go through what I had been through
I've never died before....
But I imagine that it's the most peaceful sleep
To those in need of sleep, when weak has become of strength
I weep, cause strength wouldn't let me cut my wrists
Every day I survive, I lie in the face of the public
Lost my mind, now I'm just a puppet
I hear gunshots and trumpets
Hear babies gurgle with blood in their throats
Women and children choking from smoke, explosions...
Taps.... I can hear the tracks and my bones crack
I'm scared, I fear I'm constantly in danger
Everyone I've known has become a stranger and every time I'm angered
I can hear the rounds being chambered
I've never died before....
But I'd be lying to say that I haven't been trying
I've been the Lamb chasing the Lion
Thought about overdosing on meds, maybe lead and iron
I just wanted to bleed, knowing if I were to succeed
I wouldn't enjoy my triumph
That if I were to leave, my seeds would be seized by the darkness
The thought of their hardship was the hardest to swallow
Became heartless trying to harness my hardships and wallow
No path to follow, never knew if I would have tomorrow
Or how to outlast tomorrows, I was borrowing time anyway
We're all gonna die anyway, any day, I'm tired of suffering
I've never died before....
I've never died before I saw my daughter's eyes filled with disappointments
I had become abusive, tried therapeutic appointments
How can I be miserable when I enjoyed it
How can I continue to love Love when I've destroyed it
Why must I live through war with nothing to show for it
I have more blood on my hands than coins in my pocket
I'm hurting and I don't know how to stop it, knock it off

I'm tired of being hard, but forgotten how to be soft
Something is off
I've made it home in 1 piece, but somethings were lost
And it cost everything …… Why not my life
I'm without happiness or sanity, it cost me my wife
It cost me my family, my dreams
Paid me in ribbons and pins for my elbows and knees
Nothing I want, nothing I need, nothing left to make me believe
I just wanted to leave
I could use the sleep, I'm tired, my burdens heavy
I don't want to cry…. I don't want to fight no more
I've never died before…. But I'm ready
I'm ready

As fit and in shape as I may seem… I'm suffering
Suffering from Degenerative Disc Disease, Cervical Myelopathy,
Cervical Radiculitis, Spondylosis, and the all too familiar
Carpal tunnel and arthritis – and I just work through the pain
What was once a bunch of big fancy words for
Pinched nerves, compressed spine, bad discs, and soreness
has been progressively worsening and closing curtains
I mean, I like to fight Holmes…
I like to write poems
But my bones are impeding my progress, and I'm just
Fading away, wasting my days as it feels like bits
and pieces breaking away as the body decays – and the hard part
The hard part is handling the Hellman's
Honestly – cause you can't pop the top with your wrists locked, that shits embarrassing
yet… the part that hurts isn't the pain…
it's the activities you gotta give up
the babies you can no longer pick up, when it pains you just to get up
yet sleep finds no comfort – that shit is depressing
it messes with you –
I doctor the stressing by counting my blessings,
While I still have all my digits
I'm not dead, I'm broken and looking for ways to fix it
Looking for remedies to remedy the injuries, I used to
Envy me physically – where for others I had sympathy
Is now replaced with self-pity – emptiness
With no resolve in the Tylenol, no improvement of motion from the Motrin
It toys with your emotions… motivation escaping
A painter – who can no longer hold his brush
An architect, who can no longer build, has to yield
Creating the creations of his imagination
That shit is aggravating
It hurts to smile, when the PTSD ain't killing me
Stuck between the fear of the walls closing in
And the fact that I'm losing the ability to push them back when they do
Try to run away, avoid the pain, but it hurts to put on my shoes
I used to want another child, but if I can't open the Gerber, change a diaper
How can I be responsible for another life
I was more guilty of thinking some people just complained too much
When in fact they strained too much, inflamed
And pained to the touch – and it's not a weakness…
This, you can't "mind over matter" when everything that matters
In your mind shatters – and you can't gather the will
Or muster the strength to heal – faster

You can't peel bananas – there's a hurt, with no anesthesia
Would you rather suffer from amnesia or paraplegia?
Either way, you're a burden to those that need ya
There's something about a child saying. "Daddy it's too heavy"
And all you can say is, "I know baby, we'll get it later" –
That'll make you hate yourself – now you got to wait for yourself
Or some outside help from someone else,
when you're used to being that someone else
I used to think that "falling apart was better than going to pieces"
Now that I'm falling apart, I'm going to pieces
I used to have trouble sleeping, now when I'm sleeping
I need to wear hand/arm braces that cause me trouble sleeping
I used to cry writing the poems cause I feel them deep in my soul
Now I cry when I write poems, cause of the pain deep in my bones
A glutton for punishment… I guess pain in my neck, knees, arms, hands and back
This is not a complaint, in fact… I have a favor to ask
When you get the chance, shake hands, hug your loved ones
While they physically, have the ability, to hug you back

I woke up…. Gun in one hand, blood on the other
I swear I love her
But I struck her in my sleep
Screaming while dreaming and unleashed this demon
She – afraid to get close to me, trying to Soldier me
Her biggest burden and she can't shoulder me when these things take over me
This is how the PTSD thing was told to me, it took control of me
She's supposed to be home with me, holding me
Rather be alone, she fears my tone – choose a side
Most of my peers are gone – suicide
She's got nightmares of her own, and I've become one
I'm the boogie man she runs from – Dumb-Dumb
I don't even know where this anger comes from, but I'm unstable
The VA say, I'm mentally disabled
Like incapacitated, deactivated
But I only understand being aggravated and agitated
I keep getting vaccinated, drugged
I just want them to pull the plug
Disable, disarm – deal death directly down from the Heavens
Sever these ties
I'm tired of breathing
Cheating at life since I've beat on my wife
I've done this once or twice, twice too many, no coward in me
But neither any control or recollection
Now she sleeps with weapon for protection from her protection
I'm an infection, a plague
I'm surprised she stayed
I'm surprised she forgave the way I behaved
Like when she lied to the kids about the bruises on her ribs
And the other things I never knew I did
I just blackout, then pass out when asked to put the trash out
My mind is a glasshouse – fragile
Throwing stones at the inner walls
Cause no one no longer comes when I call – it's empty
My head, my house
She's dead, my spouse – she bled
She said, I said, I screamed
I dream of gunfire and brimstone
I dream of fighting to bring my friends home
I dream of dreaming I can get my old life back
I dream that God will send my wife back
I dream they never took my kids from me
I'm praying, but I know that God don't want to hear from me
A loss of control turned into the loss of my soul

33

I was no longer whole after the holes, dig me a hole
I'm ready to go home......
I'd kill me if I knew what I did, left bruises on my Rib's ribs
Flashbacks of having to blast back, shooting at kids
The killings of women and children, an American Hero, Family Villain
I just want to take these boots off, put down my rifle
They don't know pain and sacrifice like I do
Yet every full moon, my mind becomes where-wolves-hide
I'm a monster, there's an imposter in the mirror
Empty house... I can hear the floor boards creak
I still hear her voice in my sleep... screaming
I woke up with a gun in one hand and blood on the other – dreaming...
Just another nightmare that I can't explain just how real it felt
Out of fear, I've come here... cause I need help
Being saved from myself

Blessed is 6 winters, same jacket
When you could be in that straight jacket
Keeping that anger managed, minimal damage from the savage in you
Cause even you've been ravaging you
Learning to control it, find focus, having a habit of making magical moments
Blessed is feeding your mind when your stomach empty
Staying in line when those falling behind are trying to get me, tempt me
It's moving forward when the forfeit is more tempting
Blessed is, used to being suicidal, but finding no false idols with as big a purpose as I do
It's being lied to, cheated, but not easily defeated
It's not having love when you want it, but it finding you when you need it
Finding something to believe in when you find your faith leaving
When you're aching, ain't sleeping,
Lying awake, awaiting the demons that thought they had you beaten
When there's wheezing in your breathing, yet you keep reaching
When you feel so much God in your veins, there's Jesus in your semen
It's finding reason and meaning to your being after being confused
It's walking another 100 miles, same shoes
Blessed is finding the Gospel after you've sung the Blues
Blessed is bleeding and bruising, no idea what I'm doing
But I ain't losing
No longer lost in the language, though I ain't fluent
When I ain't moving, Divine hands hold me when it's cold
Mold me – out of stone, I am the Throne
Don't always know about a next meal,
But I know that standing on the ledge feel, close to the edge feel
Fear of dying replaced by a fear of hiding, now I feel like fighting
I am.. for-ever, so I've started writing
Blessings etched in stone, bone and chromosome
Blessed is fear of the unknown, yet seeking to understand
The ability to go to war with inner demons even though I'm undermanned
Knowing you carry the world on your shoulders to free up your hands
At times your heart gets lonely to free up your plans
It's when your thoughts get blurry, and you find time for prayer
It wasn't until them dragons came at me, that I found out I'm the slayer
Even when stripped of my armor, I've found another layer
When life rips through my flesh, there's all God up under there
Sometimes I stare… at emptiness just to realize how full I've come to be
Tried grabbing onto the horns anytime the Bull would come for me
Blessed is finding no one to comfortably comfort me comforting
Cause comfort ain't what I need, I seek covenant
Blessed is walking through hell and loving it
Wondering what else these devils are coming with

Blessed is finding your way to Fatherhood via the Mothership
It's when your Futures are all admiring your presence
My children are my blessings
It's the lessons exchanged between both joy and pain
It's missing where you aimed, but never losing the target
It's finding the light when the darkness hits its hardest
The ability to chase the dreams that seem the farthest
It's having the will to see it through, even when you have nothing to start with
Blessed is the promise kept, those times you've wept over messes and wreckage
Blessed is knowing every weapon formed failed
That even in failure you prevailed, just earned a tale to tell
A trial to teach from, pain to preach from
Blessed is this beating heart and articulate tongue
In spite of this broken body, bludgeoned and numb
Having the ability to run, but lacking the desire
Having the fire, the fuel
Blessed is having the fight in you, finding the light in you right when you need it
Believing, leaving it to God when it's hard
When it scars and scabs, when it gets bad
When you feel like giving up
It's the 2nd time falling down those steps, 3rd time getting up
Though I've been knocked down, it's the strength I've found when I most needed rest
Thought I'd exhaled my last breath and began to succumb to the stress
It's the fact that I ain't dead yet
That reminds me…
That I am blessed

~When I felt like a stranger
SHE made me comfortable
In my own skin~

They said, "The foundation has been weakened"
I ain't been sleeping right
I used to dream at night
Now I'm a means to bring our means to light
At times it's script, scribble and scribe Life
Birth through pages
Never do this for the lime-lights
but the burst on stages
Bring the Church to Pagans,
The truth to Seekers and non-believers
Sometimes you got to be the voice of the Speakers
Backbone of the Leaders
Got to stretch the roots through the gravel from the seedlings
You got to remove ceilings and bring a healing when dealing with doubt
Trust in thyself that you can figure it out
Even in doubt, you got to know you're right
You must be certain with the obvious and obscure alike
Masses must believe that you'll steer them right
Been watching as the World darkens
I keep my swords sharpened
Many claim that Truth hurts, so we keep these words hardened
Details are gory behind every story of glory
Performing poorly, surely would have history repeated
After every enemy is defeated, we'll have his story deleted
I fight when energy is depleted and my stomach is empty
Fight from within the crosshairs of my enemy, knowing he'll miss me
Legends never die, when I'm gone no one should miss me
if they were listening
I'm the Message passing through, visiting
I'm visioning
Hard work and long hours, Marathon Man against Minute Men
Limitations unlimited, if you're gifted, then you give it then
Some do this for Ends, needs and Dividends
I do this to end the need for dividends
Reparations and refunds in the form of education and wisdom
Stacking the type of chips that'll reboot the system
Though tired, I stopped thinking about sleeping, started thinking about awakening
the neighbors that wreak of enslavement
Taking over the Big House from the attic to the basement
I lay awake making arrangements
Trying to remind our masses about the Kings and the Pharaohs
When their tunnel-vision narrows
Awaken the Sheep, herd the cattle
Another one entering the chamber as soon as one exits the barrel

I stay woke to admonish
there's too much work to accomplish, hurt to abolish
Got to remind mine that they have a purpose to acknowledge
This is a warzone not a playground
I won't lay down or lay round, they've found a way to conquer and confuse
A way to control and abuse
Pain be our fuel, just help me to build our tools and use them
Forward momentum moving toward improvements
Away from the ruins; project apartments
Apart meant segregated, Apart meant separated
That darkness left us devastated
Experiments like Syphilis is how they medicated
Slaughtered Natives while engaged in prayer as they meditated
Tarnished or taken everything sacred, renamed it
And When Hate called you a Nigga, you claimed it
What your name is
Monkey see, Monkey do, Nigga look just like you
What your aim is
Where your brain is
Claiming more kids in these streets than you do on your taxes
Drive-bys and accidents
Forced on us mass incarceration and you're cooperating
Can't claim to be innocent if your actions aren't corroborating
What side are you on
Are you King, or you pawn
More of a part of the problem of why the Fathers are gone
We can either think or become extinct
Stabilize or collapse
Wear the Crown or drown, put the Proud back in the Black
Royal in how we act, loyalty to the pack
I don't sleep cause I got to teach, I got goals and people to reach
Coma patients to awaken with these pictures I'm painting
Prisoner unchaining with every sentence I'm saying
The messages I'm relaying,
Keep a record of my thoughts so the music keeps playing
Spread my light, shine like the Sun
Knowing I need not fall to rise like one
...Good Morning,
.....I got work to do.

I only speak when spoken to
Cause I disapprove of your vernacular
Life is a game of inches
And I'm trying to avoid the tacklers
Heaven is a Woman
And I've found a way to capture her, I imagined her
She had scars from hell, I just took the time to bandage her
Paradise for my daughters, the way I father them
Make me a martyr, 'fore I let America swallow them
Their light shines bright like they are halogen
Their Black is beautiful, lips don't need no collagen
I tell them, "Knowledge begins where college ends"
Easiest way to find sin is to follow trend
Learn to lead baby, you don't need to follow men
Still gotta keep your head up in the shallow end
Seek and you shall find, the deepest depths of my mind woven into the rhymes I left behind
Every line was designed to hide the signs
Never forget the Pharaohs, the keys were kept with the Kings
They told us how to speak, but from the soul we learned to sing
I ain't trying to be on some Black/White
I just got proof that the truth usually shines with a black-light
A sharp tongue will force your train of thought to jackknife
Make your back pike, skin crawl and all
Talking about how they did us wrong when we were strong
And we've been believing in them all along
Nah, this ain't one of them Jesus speeches from the Preachers
This ain't some old Negro thesis about how they used to treat us
This is the food for thought you need to eat to nourish the mind of your fetus
We're more than we've been
Hatred made mortals of men
Even if I could be born once again, I'll never lay down my Brown
They can "Off" my head, but never lay down my Crown
Yeah, it gets dangerous when the endangered are angered
That picture painted is tainted
They can't explain it so they blame it on spaceships
But I've seen God, thick hips and cellulite
Met devils who'll purchase your soul, imprison you just to sell you life, any cell you like
Been trying to live right, it's been 1 hell of a fight
I mean, we're just trying to live......right
The only constant is the unconscious claiming to be woke while living the American Dream
Maybe they misspoke, everybody ain't as woke as they seem

40

Cut from different cloths, but the same cheap fabric stitched into the seams
Maybe that's why they're still sagging, got that baggage in their genes
From getting bagged on the Ave, with them baggies in your jeans
To watching Rappers, Athletes and Actors getting body-bagged for sipping that lean
Then we do the same
There's a difference between the cards you're dealt and the hand that's played
They've been feeding you stuffing when nothing was in the stomach
But nothing of substance was in the stuffing
Helping hands extended from a man grinning, knowing he's bluffing
I'm trying to teach the Brothers who don't know how to use their weapon
Train my Sisters who've been abused and never felt protected
She don't know she's a blessing
Been led to misread the message

Wrong time, wrong place…
I almost fell, know I should've bailed
Cost me an overnight in a cell in jail
Face swells and the smell of hell
Momma always said to make better decisions
Or end up dead or imprisoned, I should've listened
I thought she was tripping, never be on a milk box missing
Be without a pot to piss in
I was raised on the "Never get caught snitching" or slipping
I bought bricks to pitch for figures, I figured
Them digits would've did it for me
Know no one would go get it for me
Now look how freely I give my freedom – Homie listen
Bad infections hamper vision, damage positions
A lack of precision leads to bad collisions
When you're in the driver's seat – why compete
When you're not complete.
Watch your feet when trying to fill shoes that don't belong to you
Something's wrong with you if you let peer pressure measure the man in you
You tie your hands when you band with the Band that pushes grams for bands
You really don't understand young man
I was a young man, dumb plans, gun in hand
Through Philadelphia streets I ran like Cunningham
Train stations straight to Brooklyn, I was booking
Looking over my shoulder
Pockets filled with all I had stolen
Now I'm older, nothing to show for it
Some cats I did dirty in Jersey wanna murk me
They really wanna hurt me
Jokers who were posers pretending to be friends began to desert me
I was lonely, no homies, even lost touch with the homies that owe me
They act like they don't know me
Heartless, they don't want no parts of this
I left that darkness, went from God less
To catching God's lift, I should've listened
When my Elder said to make better decisions
I remembered as soon as I became a member of a correctional facility
Silly me
Now I see what happens when acting like someone who ain't really me
Now they ration what I eat, ration how much I sleep
All because my rationale was weak, I wasn't thinking properly
Until I became state property, inmate – proud of me???
Nah, old friends clowning me, cellmates crowding me
Tears drowning me after each charge came down on me

Finally free but the damage is done
When I was young, I swear I was having some fun
At least I've learned blessings and lessons to pass on to my son
Son… sinning ain't winning – listen
You want to make a better living
Start by making better decisions

~SHE asked for the truth
I spoke to HER of my love
Lust and my feelings~

For a couple of years now, I've been doing her laundry…
Helping to unpack her closet of the nonsense
Getting rid of the shit – she can no longer fit
Not cause she's gotten thick – cause she's gotten thick
Fit in them hips, learned to punch and kick cause she's gotten hit
War drove her wardrobe to scorned, closed
I could have sworn Rose wore thorned clothes
She wasn't born with those – silenced; mouth closed
But when she unzipped her lips, she adorned with prose
She didn't know… that she was the Sun, dressed
Sashayed, cascades and flows; that she glows
But I'd seen her strength in the very seam of her genes
Cause her Momma-Queen mean; self-esteem in the teens on that 10-scale
Tell she's been broken, but she mends well
I've been folding clothes, giving her closure
She was holding boulders, looking over her shoulders
Trying to watch her back, now she can drop that and relax cause I'm the strap
She used to dress in all black, afraid of colors
Cause some motherfuckers wanted to color
I've had to take down those hangers, cause she just wanted to tie-dye
Sleeveless… she'd just… wrap in the arms of Jesus
Hoping to leave this – escape this – "Why did God create this? I hate this"
Those statements, I've stored boxes of briefs in the basement
I've seen her naked – unveiled
That smile, she used to fake it
Now head – dressed, trained, crowned, I look at her make it
I look at her sacred, her blues been used
Her hues no longer bruise
Sometimes the ugliest baggage reveals the prettiest package
She was covered in pain, and I've been scrubbing through stains
Mud stains, blood stains – love Gains Aim no matter how high the Tide
You rise to meet it, we're perfectly pleated – bound
Our doubled helix wound
As if the universe meant us thrown together
Sometimes we seem stressed (seamstress), but we've been sewn together
I had to show her – now you'll never have to worry about your him (hem) falling out of place
Wing cling to feather for protection from the elements
I know it takes more than her donning my coat-of-arms to render that need irrelevant
Cause though there will always be things left in her closet that'll rob her of joy
I'll always be there to jack it
I've got a habit - of folding clothes
And no matter how many socks come up missing

Where she's come from is something I'm never forgetting
I've got a habit of folding clothes
I saw the fabric where holes arose (in Courtney Rose)
Where it began to corrode and mold, it would barely hold…
Somethings are too delicate to be permanently pressed
Over each mess we mesh like flesh to bone
Love hard – stone washing away fears and tears
That I'll be replacing with years of cheers
For the times she wasn't shown her house is home
She now has a throne to own, she knows, she shares that
No longer wears that alone, she knows…
That our story's next chapter won't damper
And I'm about to throw onesies in her hamper
I've learned… so much about the past her
That every unanswered question, I can already answer
I used to smell her hurt in the filth
Until covering her with my quilt of affection
I recognized infection in her demeanor first time I'd seen her
I keep her cheekbones dry, cleaner than ever
This ain't fair weather
or for whether-or-not her colors ever bleed again…
Not the way I'm treating them
Keeping them wrapped in blessings, the love she's dressed in
Got her wearing me out…
I've been doing laundry, washing away the dirt from former
Now that light shining... And I'm in love with the way it looks on her

She said that she used to be depressed....
Told me that the stress, had her a lot bigger
She said, she'd lost about 150 lbs.
I said, "Oh.... You've finally cut off that useless Nigga"
She said, receiving compliments wasn't something she was used too
I said, it's hard to swallow with so much on your plate
When your relation's situation is in bad shape, you'll start to lose you
I told her, I ain't one for adding to your baggage
I'm sure you got some burdens I can help you carry
A couple of worries I can help you bury
She said, I hope you'll never see the me I used to be
I said, those who were blessed with your presence and thought lesser
Must've had their vision blurry
She said that she was a Big Girl....
And I replied, "Well, they cry too"
Days of your past, shaded blue, we'll never Déjà vu
You've always been you, no matter how they'd view
You've lost a couple pounds, gained sex appeal and confidence
Trimmed to a slimmer figure, speaks volumes of your accomplishments
It's common sense, you've been surrounded by Bad Guys and their Accomplices
You're standing before a Man....... Maybe for the first time
And this Man has a different definition of "Fine"
You can't squeeze a dollar out of a Dime, pay that no mind
I'm trying to get into your mind, I'm trying to find my future in your behind
Embrace the spine that connects the two
I'm trying to become the lifeline you're connected too
I can tell that the last dude neglected you
Until even you started rejecting you
Beautiful, doesn't begin to describe
You are Biblical Scribe, Lost language
Maybe when life had you beat, you'd eat yourself to sleep
Love-life grew sour, so you searched for something sweet
Maybe it's genetics, but he made you feel pathetic
But He and Me are two separate people, we aren't equals
Maybe he just didn't see you
Maybe he noticed your Hip and Thigh size but not your eyes
Maybe he missed your grace by being too concerned with your waistline
Maybe he didn't know how to walk with you or talk to you
Maybe he couldn't please you the way that chocolate do
Maybe the Bitch in him is what made him bark at you
-She lowered her gaze
I said, "Look at me when I talk to you!"
She said, she used to be ashamed, a little socially awkward too
I asked her, what happened to make this bashful you

She said, she was battered, bruised, had scattered views of everything she had shattered through
I said, believe me when I tell you....
You're more than worth your weight in gold
You're more than the stories of old he told when scolding that you still hold on to
Never let the opinions of others mold you
Push-ups and Sit-ups aren't as impressive as your Stand-up
Pick your head up, I know you're fed up
But just like you, I got an appetite too
Everything is on the menu, but I only want You.

She feels like home....
Like, you know you've found a Queen when she feels like Throne
She's all I think or dream of, it feels like dome
My art was born from pain, but with her...
I don't know how I still write poems.... This is foreign to me
As if the Father figured four evers wasn't long enough of a life
He sent me a piece of heaven and said, "This, is how you choose a wife"
My 'up all nights' have been replaced by being up all night
3am used to be reserved for nightmares, cold-sweats and anxiety
Now, if I happen to be awake, there's an Angel laying there beside of me
I've found peace – for my trauma, found sleep – for the insomnia
Found that 7 years is a long time to wait, but it was well worth it, deserving of a
better treasure
The weather always takes us where we need to be, lost and found
I've been tossed around, I've lost somethings costly
Handled things awfully, at my own pace, never learned to wait
And I know 'haste makes waste,' yet the weights are finally lifted
His Greatness has finally gifted me with vision
I was in a prison I built myself – 4 walls came tumbling down
I used to talk about pain, I'm just mumbling now – I've found....
That Honey is sweeter than sugar and better for your health
That it ain't the glare of the diamonds not crystals but the Rose of the ruby that
holds true wealth
And she feels like....
5 prayers a day, forgiveness and fasting – like, all that is holy
She holds me, she molds me like she knows me
Like she knows we closely imitate creation, this is God's work
That...'Faith without prayer is dead'...
Well my hands are dirty and I've never felt more alive
Peaches and sunshine are all we need to survive sometimes
But I've found an energy, a light that I don't have to fight
I don't have to fake, hide or run from, there's no more conundrum
Just brilliant colors covering the canvas of my Black World...
Books can't tell this story with a thousand pics, a million words
Both our hearts have been broken, feels like I perfectly fill hers
Starving and empty, she feeds me life, I fill in her
Though the outskirts of our palace may be shrouded by cowards and malice...
She's ready for any challenge, keeps me balanced, driven
Together we are pump and piston
People perceive, poke, pry and pontificate, pushing problems
But I feel that we are par for the course
Breakups, mistakes, hatred, divorce –
Heartache, heartbreak, pain-stricken, abuse – recluse
You need to get used to you after being used to being used

Maybe I'm making a fool of myself, but I'm a fool for love
I'm being schooled by love
I know Dopamine means,
This love in my heart, travels to the other parts every time her voice is heard
Like when she calls me "Big Boy," though I'm 'Fair in Height'
Which means she melts ... every time my touch is felt, I ain't no dummy,
I just turn to putty in the arms of the woman that wants me as much as she loves me
And she feels like....
I've repeated the same mistakes so often, I can't possibly be wrong again
When it's 7 years before you've belonged to them, that you belonged to them
That may have been too long for them cause experiences made you wrong for them
But you gotta learn to swim when your head's down or you'll surely drown
Drowning is scary.... feels like dying
She is life and she feels like flying
I now know how it feels to flutter by butterflies
I don't wonder why I'm lightheaded....
I'm more focused on where we're headed
She feels like, going places, onyx and golden bracelets
She feels like, something that feels right...when it's done right
She feels like.... Momma your son finally found his Sunlight
And all that matters are our Venus, Mars and Saturn
When your anus ain't in our business, you can witness the magic
And.... I don't even believe in magic
But I've been saying my prayers since prayers asked for me to get here
I know blessings....
I've waited in long line after long line, jumped in the wrong line at the wrong time
But my God is always 'on time'
She feels like.... be patient....
Like.... keep waiting, greatness takes time to find
She feels like.... She was always supposed to be .. and will be....
Mine

Most men just want to make you climax…
My intention's to listen to every sentence mentioned
And turn the pages on all of the stages from your beginning you should be forgetting
Your table of contents shows heartache, anger, pain & despair
Headaches… maybe that's why you keep changing your hair
I will bring more to the table than contents
And I got enough to share – with you I can make movies
You move me with your script
Your lips part and art spills from your lips
Hips part when it's dark and I'm seeing the spark betwixt your hips
The sun in your eyes and I'd be lying to deny that I'm trying
To scribe my son through your thighs
My space was empty… until you filled it
I owe you this world that I'm building
Turn the page… better days await
Allow me to give you a home where laughter hangs from the rafters
Love in the oven, be my woman
These streets be passion woven – stitched and sewn
Come sit in this throne, home is where the heart is
You've already been shown what apart meant –
Let's come together forever and never part ties
I got you during the hard times
Almost 30 chapters in, no bookmark needed, I'm still reading
Still having a hard time believing that I'm not dreaming
I'm breathing better, you can't measure that
Dark clouds from your past, but I can weather that
Whether that be the abuse or misuse, lie and excuse
That you've grown used to, grown used to how people used you
Some of the best parts of you have been shut down, I'm down to reboot you
When you're tapped out, let me refuel you
Let me assure you, this is so pure, I could bleed, cry and pour you
Your pain is flowing through my veins
I'm trying to suck you dry every time we touch – you and I
We're made for balance – I accept the challenge of repairing the damage
Being the bandage, the healing
Soft to the touch, sensitive to your feelings
Yet still I have you climbing the ceilings, peeling paint off the walls
All life long, show you that strong…
Doesn't have to mean abrasive when embracing
I've read the harsh things that have been written
So ready to forget them while I'm erasing, be patient…
I'll replace them with something amazing, turn the page
At this stage, you don't know who to trust

I know, from the dude who lusted you to the fool who busted you up
Just wanting their nuts, didn't know how to touch your soul
I know… Baby let that go –
Let me give you something worth holding, no withholding
Let me show you what it feels like when no one's controlling
Unfold your arms, I won't harm you
Being loved shouldn't alarm you – I am not you
We were both found drowning in tears, and I couldn't swim
Now it feels like I'm walking on waves, turn the page
Light some frankincense and sage – allow your every page to be filled
Quran's scriptures, Biblical text and sacrifice – my ink will be spilled
Let me author your authorship, have your hand in handling the heart
Properly – show me that my Property … is Real Estate
Make no mistake, you won't have to Shake away from
Love, there's a difference between Real and fake love
And we've got a great love pending…
I don't even want to finish,
Forever stuck between your chapter as if every word you utter
Is only the beginning

…Turn the page
You'll always find me there

I give all praises to Him, cause I've found you
I'm crazy about you
Lose you, let you go…. I ain't about to
Baby, I'm all about you, hope you never doubt
Though trying times lay ahead, I'm sure we'll work them out
I know that nothing is perfect….
Short of you and our Creator, Maker, our Savior
For you I am forever in debt
Cause I know He has me in His favor
You should never feel less than, for you are the blessing
I may not be the best man
But you got the right one
I can't sing you a song, but I'll learn how to write one
Stand firm when the fights come
We won't always be happy, but you'll always have me
I don't promise you, I promise God for the gift that He gave me
For how rich that He made me, when He gave me you
When my praying for a miracle and my dreams came true
And though I'm scared, I'm prepared for the disagreements
Things won't always be convenient, at times indecent
But you'll never know mistreatment
Never let you forget what we meant
I value you like the most valuable valuable that man can give value too
I love you to the core, I more than adore
There's no one I love more, I'm sure, I'm certain
You are picture perfect
And I'm hurting cause I can't give you a perfect person
But Baby I'm worth it, I'm working
Hoping I can keep you smiley faced, your neck laced
And your body draped in passionate kissing and hugging, intense loving
Let me apologize ahead of time for my shortcomings
Say, "I'm sorry for being human," but Baby, few men can love like I can
If only I knew then what I know now
I would have found you, loved you back when I was a child
Molded you out of Play-doh, built you a castle out of Legos
Mastered Nintendo's cheat code
Up-down-up-down-left-right-left-right-B-A-B-A-Select-Start
So that I could spend the next 30 lives giving you my heart
Cause 1 lifetime- clearly goes too fast
And I gotta make us last, I gotta make up for your past
I gotta make a way to give you what you've never had
Baby, you deserve your own culture, language and Natives
Cause you've mothered Nature
I've seen the Sun shine like you do

And it always rains like you do
My love-life was almost dead, prepared to jump out the window
Then look at what the wind blew....
I love you more than life,
Make sure when I'm gone that my headstone reads
"He loved God, Children, and then You"
I can't even understand a love like this, I just pretend to
But in you I have a friend who.........................
I have a love that's....................................
And Baby I'm just...................................
I'm just speechless.

Sorry for the interruption, but I had to say something.

I've never played with Barbie Dolls, wasn't raised to do so
not into plastic parts, hearts or pose-able limbs
Not attracted to the over accessorized diamonds and gems
or a Woman that thin...
I want something plump to bump into
full course meals on the menu
high heels only when I'm in you, so I can bend you perfectly
enter you inversely,
submerging me into the depths of your wettest of flesh
I need love handles to grip when I'm slipping in
A Love that handles my grip, when I'm slipping
She listens when I mention every intention and decision
Wisdom is accepted and reciprocated
minds are titillated
I mean she gotta be real to me
She gotta feel me, the real me, be able to heal me
deal me better hands, when life calls my bluff
she gotta like it rough,
but be able to smooth my edges, hold true to our pledges
She gotta be confident beyond fake breasts and hair pieces
knowing I don't care where her hair reaches
I want a Woman... whose best parts are her stretch marks...
She don't need to be shaped like an hourglass
I'm trying to count the grains of intensity in her past
See the struggles she's been overcoming
I want a Woman
I want to argue for the thrills of losing the goose-bumps and chills
Just to know our Love is Real
That's hard to do when she ain't
When she fake, then we break,
cause she can't keep her back straight from carrying this weight
I want a Woman with weight...in her thighs
I can tell she'll wait, in her eyes
A woman that cries, cause Big Girls still do
I want a Big Girl, who can eat for two
when life throws us lemons...
She be into fruit salads while I'm tossing hers
She ain't sucking her teeth when she slurs her words
and we exchange our gifts cause we deserve, never mind our last nerves
I don't want that fake and phony
cold when she hold me
better off lonely
cause she didn't give she just loaned me, but don't owe me
don't go her way for a day, that night she don't know me

Boney, no body to hold onto…
Like really, she's Nobody to hold onto
I want a Woman who's handling the baggage she's carried
but ain't afraid to be carried and down to be married
I don't need a Doll who's gonna dog me, leap frog to the next John when I'm wrong
She gotta be strong and hold on, get a long for the haul
I want a woman whose feet hurt from walking, but still a sweetheart when talking
She ain't calling me names
we don't add on to the pain by playing games
I want that Love that's tangible
Love that's manageable
I want a Woman that can throw blows if ever I'm being handled
I need a Real Woman, a Whole Woman, to be my sole Woman
I mean be my Soul Woman
I want a Big Girl
cause I'm tired of little whiny-ass Jezebels and Divas
Whose self-worth only amounts to their physical features
I want a Woman that makes me feel protected
a Woman I can play Chess with, mind tested
be Blessed with
I must admit……
I love them thick
the kind of thick that Barbie ain't dressed with
She gotta know her 'Thick' she was blessed with
She looks her best in
That 'Thick' that makes me lick lips and kiss every inch
a thick I can pinch and make a wish to be Rich
then make her remind me I am, by calling my name
I want a woman perfectly made for Lovers with bad aim
Cause I don't want to miss Her
A Picture….
too much to be framed or contained in pretty wrapping for marketing
like the type of dames so many Lames seem to be targeting
My argument is simple
I want a Woman with Ass-dimples and a gut
Big butt and flaws in her strut
A Woman who ain't interested in Ken nor Milton Bradley
She ain't silicon adding, when her breasts get saggy
and instead of getting naggy, she helps me find the way how
I've never played with Barbie
and I ain't about to start now.

She's about 5 foot-fine, golden in complexion, pure heaven
Keeps my love swollen with erections, sexual perfection
She's the exception to perfection
Dressed in blessings, flesh, skin and melanin
She's like....
A freshly toasted English Muffin, honey-butter
Apple jelly on both sides
She don't just run through my thoughts, she glides
She butterflies my insides, and when I'm inside
She cascades and flows
Trembles when she cums, sashays when she goes
Hey hips be hypnotizing, thighs thick
She's fit, the perfect size, back-end wide
Eyes alluring, she be having my sweat pouring
Nights I've slept snoring, ignoring the fatigue
From how she loves me to my knees
She came at a time when I didn't believe, I need love...
She's not my dream girl, she's the girl dreams are made of
And I just want to brag about her
I be doing bad without her
I had a fear of drowning before she snatched me from my tears
I would collapse, she said fight back, now I'm attacking what I fear
She's the total package, dragging her baggage in the rear
Made me the Dragon I couldn't imagine when the passion wasn't there
She's nasty with the care
She rides for us both, I'm just a passenger on the Mare
She's God-like, like equivalent to omnipotent
If anything in life were perfect, she invented it
She's that Coffee brown,
Hot, strong and black
That fresh oysters and chocolate, that aphrodisiac
Black Aphrodite, her smile is moonshine and lightning
And I'm just scratching the surface, she's perfect
She's perfect even beneath the surface
Sweet enough to eat, so I be feasting beneath the cervix
I don't just put it down.... I wear her like a crown
In her rainfall, I'm ready to drown every time she comes around
When she wants it rougher and harder
She just fucks me like karma
She doesn't get excited, our fuse is always already ignited
We sear and scorch when she lights the torch
She holds me down, while I hold down the fort
Lifts me up when I'm slipping, like we're sharing the same vision
And every time our hearts speak, our bodies listen

There ain't no fission, this is fusion, no confusion
I may not always feel like I'm winning, but she makes sure I never feel like I'm losing
I'm sure heaven lost its blueprint
She's the black ink on the white lie, one of a kind
Mankind wasn't meant to be perfect, she's the first of Womankind
She came to me in a storm, then my life transformed
I call her Voluptuous Prime
I be trying to nickel and dime her time
Cause it never makes sense to leave her vicinity
I keep my arms locked on her like the rings around infinity
Perfect eight, I mean perfect shape, weight and taste
And I throw no shade when I say, "Babe is the perfect shade"
That Ebony complexion perfection
That Heavenly reflection perfection
Like God used her image as inspiration to create the Heavens
I mean, her Mother must've been the messenger cause she's the message
Perfection…. No greater reference than this vestige
She's perfection perfected
I mean, even the pain from my past, I've learned to accept it cause I believe that she's worth it
And if that's a lie, then I've already died and gone to heaven cause…
She's perfect

The Moon… only appears to shine from the Sun's reflection
And just like that, from those Heavenly blessings I've never need protection
Love… you should have never been used as a weapon
Formed against you, it was never meant to
Now you've got issues to get through
I've been through some shit too, but I had to get through to get you
To get due –
I've missed you before we met
I hadn't even gotten to know you yet,
Before tears made cheek-bones wet, before the sweat of sex
Before I dealt with neglect or disrespect, before I began to accept less
I mean I used to think heartbreak was normal before you
Before you, everything ended tragic, before you I never believed in magic
Until you happened to happen
I've been having dreams
In which happiness happened but I never imagined
Capturing dragons – excuse me….
I'm still having a hard time believing as you are seeing
What your – being with me means to me
You are a miracle and a half, I need no convincing
Listen to me with your heart…
We are music, poetry, beauty and art
We don't make love; love makes you and I
Before you, I only knew care, concern and lust
Before you, stands a man you can trust
Before you, I've now found a fantasy I can touch
Baby I still got a crush, I still got to clutch and pray
Loss for words, but still have so much to say
We've both had what we thought was love decay, become afraid
We stayed, but now a path has been paved
A foundation has been laid for us to be saved
I know it's hard being brave
Trying to stave off what you've gotten used to
Trying to stray away from the usual
Beautiful scars are the ones behind us, the ones that rewarded us
That we're survivors, I wasn't sent to hurt you
Sworn to my Creator as well as the Goddess who birthed you
I'm not here to take advantage or to damage you more
Been trying to prove through my actions that my intentions are pure
I ain't ever been more sure before
You feel like the cure for every war I've endured
And Baby I'm dying trying to cure every war of yours…
Every time I kneel to pray or bow my head to say grace, I see your face
Like God's way of telling me you're the answer

God is telling me that you're the fix
God has been telling me to stop searching, God assured me that this is it
And I don't argue with God
Nor will I deny the blessing earned from lessons learned
Now that I've learned to discern, the real from the fake
What heals from what aches and what builds from what breaks
There's no mistaking this, no making this up
Imagine waking up in Heaven's embrace and staring into the Sun,
Finding beauty in her blemishes
It's like tracing your grace creates calligraphy from my penmanship
Stars sparkle, the Moon… shine
And I've been living life… since you've been mine
I love the way you Rise

And I'm ready to bask in your glow for a lifetime

~SHE had been betrayed
We had shared similar pain
Scars began to fade~

I remember....
You were there when I was feeding you
But disappeared when I needed you
On Facebook seeing you
When I should've deleted you...
My guess, I needed fuel to burn
I had to be a fool to learn
But that's what I get for giving a love you never earned
Thought I had a gift to discern
We were breaking bread, I was the Baker
Swear on my Maker, I never saw you as a faker
I suppose I was blinded by the make-up
Like a Band, our bond went through a breakup
When you became a dick from the waist up
Thought I'd wait up for you to shape up
Stayed on your team, even took the pay cut
But then your Hate struck
Like you ain't know to get your weight up before you try and roll Shake up
Hate what it's come to
Hate what we've gone through
Hate that I had to replace the safe space I had to run to
Swore this was a family we belonged to
I read that wrong too
From opening my home to giving loans
From mending souls to broken bones
From me teaching you how to build a throne
To you leaving me at the end of the road
I'm no scholar but I ain't stupid
The truth is, you used me 'til I was useless
Sad that it sounds as negative as this proof is
But I'd never pictured this
Taught you most of what you know, but I never mentored this
Thought maybe you were innocent in the incidents
I never mentioned it
I'd just get used to the friction once the tension hit
You've faded, now when I look at your picture I can see the bitch in it
The thought of you makes my skin crawl, I hate arachnids
You messed my head up more than Iraq did
Stuck in a web of deception
Thought you were the exception amongst the blood suckers
Drained me like a mother fucker
Damn liars and Vampires
I went to bat for you
Until I was stabbed in the back by you

I couldn't see you starve so I kept you eating
I was beasting while you were feasting
I took your beatings
Buying into a friendship that you were leasing
Guess I should be thankful that you released me
You made it look easy
Told my kids I want a Turn Up when I'm dead
You ain't invited to the party
Ain't because I'm broken hearted
It's because to you I'm already dearly departed
Already drifted into the darkness, been carried into the light
First time in my life, I've got my vision right
New view of the big picture, I'm the victor
Cutting my losses, made Rich richer
You tend to swear to God on your life, now die lonely
You're phony
I once felt like I took a loss, but I don't want you to owe me
Should've listened that sign of yours that read,
"Don't trust me farther than you can throw me"
It damn near broke me, sleepless nights would choke me
Dreaming of roses, pricked my finger on a thorn and it woke me
I went from hopeless, battered, broken, shattered
To piecing back the pieces that truly mattered
And all that matters are these 6 protons, neutrons and electrons
Cut out a few ex-cons, a con-artist and a shape-shifter
And things change way different
When I was just a hot line, you were my best rhyme
But now that I know better, ain't gonna be no Next Time
I remember.....
Yeah, I remember

Men Don't...
Leave women in bruises or be giving excuses of why they ain't raising their
children
We men be in to nation building, ready willing
Men don't...be crying lying about a predicament when we get
into shit
Or the freedoms we forfeit behind a fee when we wouldn't come off it
We take what is offered off the top
Live by the laws that don't involve the cops
It only gets awkward when you can't afford it
Know when to stop – My Nigga, we are not
Men don't....
Talk shit about bitches to bitches, we leave that to bitches
Men don't fuck with bitches, but build with sisters, bitches are bad business
Mad niggas are mad bitches are more man than mad niggas, niggas mad
Men don't get mad that mad niggas got 'bitch' in them
It ain't in our genes, that's 'Bitch Denim'
Men don't be scared to leave the house after running their mouth cause the Boogie
Man Out
Men, we hang out even when your money ran out
Men be there when you need us, even when you can't pay or feed us
Men don't plant seeds, a fetus, then leave us another fatherless child
Men don't remove their crowns
It's forever embedded, dreaded into our strands
It's in how we stand, how we walk
How we plan when we talk, before we embark
Men don't bark, men mend hearts, finish what we start
Men don't fear the dark, we don't prostitute our art
We do this from the heart, not for legs to part
Men don't...
Barter, trade, then leave debts unpaid
That ain't how men behave
Catch the wave, or catch a fade
Men don't play that way with their pay
Men don't brag about the shit they got when they ain't got nothing
Or the chics they've bagged when they were out nuttin', fucking
Men don't run when being confronted or hide when being hunted
Keep it 100, we be the most wanted, needed
Men don't be easily defeated, or envious that an enemy succeeded
Envy isn't needed, men don't leave your energy depleted
Men don't suppose to pose as figures, we're only supposed to pose for pictures
Men don't suppose to be niggas, niggas posing as men
Cobra's posing as friend, phonies posing as kin
Men don't do fake shit, make shit up

Know when to build, when to break shit up
Men don't...
Get bored then explore, men tour, we mentor
We're the difference between men 'Who Are' and 'Men-whores'
Men don't have to be moved by force, we are the force, we stay the course
If we take a loss, we shake it off, men don't be the boss
We be the Leaders, we be the Master Teachers
Men don't be the deceivers, our Queens need us
Men don't be leeches, we be the features, the fathers
We be what God is, the strength for our daughters
The way for our sons
Responsibility come, men don't run, we son our young and raise them
Praise them, men don't betray them
We train them, men mean them, we don't just say them
Situations, better we make them, we give them hope
Men do what the women won't
Many people become disappointments to the world
... Men don't

I don't normally do this…
But a bitch will fake a rape, say it was a mistake
Play stupid... she'll play cupid, then say she ain't wanna do it
You know, go from 'screw it, to why not screw it'
Knowing she ain't got to prove it to have somebody's life ruined
Bitches…
Bitches always mad when you don't want his bitch ass
Caught feelings like it was him you were talking to,
Started stalking you, with nothing to offer you
You just want to be his friend, his sister, but he don't get the picture,
The bitches throwing fits cause he can't get with cha
Bitches…
Bitches wanna be you, see you happy
You think they're clapping; they're waiting for something bad to happen
Phony friendship as a weapon, they wanna steal your blessing
No matter how much you blessed them, when they had less than
Bitches
Some bitches will tell your business before they sell you business
Hell of a friendship
Bitches missing edges – inches, so they're getting ig'nant
Act indignant –
Their difference are just remnants of a friendship that really ain't ever been shit
Bitches…
Bitches be crazy… bitches are jealous, spiteful
Bitches don't like you, bitches wanna fight you, cause bitches made wishes to be just like you
Bitches…
Bitches call you when they need you, mislead you, feed you bullshit
12 shells empty of a full clip, ain't that some bullshit
You'd be assed out if ever you had to pull it
Click – Click….
Bitches ain't gender specific, but consistent pretenders
They be at the center like members
Beg for your mercy and grace like sinners at dinner
Cold-hearted, gotta separate your winners from your winters
Give 'em enough time to face the embers and watch 'em splinter
Your support system limber where it should be stiff
You ain't got a Gift, you've got a trick – after all of your shit
Bitches… give them gold and won't get your Silverback
Send them roaches home and watch them slither back
You'll try to black love these bitches when they come around
Bitches be green with envy, when you're October Brown
Bitches lean on lies… not a sober sound
Bitches be trife like that, knife to back

Their nice is act, their life ain't fact
Bitches want to take credit but can't debit
Talk that shit, then swear they ain't said it
Bitches have attitudes, lack gratitude - get mad at you
When you unable to cater or favor them
Bitches want you to slave for them, even when you're
Saving them bitches
Bitches…
Bitches beg, borrow, spit, swallow, they filth wallow
They've got that dick envy, their shit empty – simply put
They ain't shit
You've got to exterminate before they permeate
Start to germinate, bitches are contagious, this strain
You've got to contain this, it's strange
We've got to rid these bitches
Stop giving those bitches life
Die bitches…
Bitches kill me, these bitches filthy
Bitches play victim well when they tell it
Bitches helpless –
Bitches have your number saved under 'Savior'
But they're strangers, they're dangerous, they're anus
They ain't just heinous – despicable, reprehensible
Some of their bullshit is unforgiveable
These bitches is everywhere –
In your hair, in your business, bitches on your friends list
Bitches on your Christmas gift list, in your prayer circle
Hearing bitches bitching in your head, we gotta stop letting
Bitches in our beds, stop repeating what bitches said
Don't trust a bitch – until the bitch in them is dead
Bitches….

Don't be surprised by the back-stabbings…
Sometimes, creatures of habit need to be subtracted
It's simple mathematics – they'll hurt you
Remove those squares from within your circle
They'll always try angles, leave you tangled in webs
Deception…. Deceitful
Most people befriend you with hopes of finding a way to defeat you….
These clowns smile in your face, but their joy is an act
They ain't loyal behind your back
Waiting for you to train-wreck, so they can tie you to the tracks….
They'll be playing it cool, waiting to see you in the hot seat
I've seen the snakes in the grass, so I keep my rose in the concrete
You were tattooing their name when they refrained from use of permanent marker
When your times got harder, their tongues grew sharper
The blade was longer, so when the rain was over, your days grew darker
You're the target
They're about to run up on you with the nonsense, the gossip, the rhetoric, the jargon
Take advantage of your goodwill and then beg for a pardon
They'll have an answer for everything, except when you're calling
Hands out, but won't catch when you're falling
You'll be putting your all in
They'll be short-changing you, changing you, hanging you to dry
Airing dirty laundry and taking you to the cleaners
They swear to God in your face, but there's demon in their demeanor
Fake, phony, flagrant, foul
More immature than the seeds you house when you feed their mouths
They'll flip – switch up on you, they're versatile
Fraudulent
They tend to miss you when abroad you trip, when they can't afford what you spent
Yesterday was beg and borrow, but they won't see you tomorrow
Never there when you need them, but you feed them when their stomachs hollow
Like they ain't got pride to swallow…
They know that you'll fend for them, they ain't in friend form
You just became the dummy they depend on
The pawn they push, they'll use you
Take what they want, then paint an ugly picture, turn around and cartoon you
They don't take you serious
You'll get your heart attacked trying to keep your heart in tact
Giving and never given back
Most times you won't even know where they be at until they relapse
Start to need you again, when in need of a friend, they got pretend in their grin

Slick, smooth – You don't see how they move
If you could shine like the Sun, they'd sell your whispers to the Moon
They are, sorry, sloppy, carbon copies - They don't really exist
They Jekyll and Hyde
They pry inside and try to divide with lies
Then they wanna beg for a ride, then they wanna beg for a dime
They wanna give you the side-eye knowing they've crossed the line
Claiming they'll ride or die, I guess these dummies are mummies
Wrapped up in your business
Can tell you everything they've heard, but none of what they witnessed
These tools are ratchet
You could give them the shirt off your back and they'll talk crap about the fabric
No friend of yours, they'll be acting -latest fashion
They're trendy – friendly enemies and pretend-to-be's
Their desire to be above you is the reason they can't love you
They hug you snug, just to open you up to get run through
They want you...... to fail
Don't be roped in with past importance
It's time to let those friendships… set sail

They know you've never wrestled with a wrestler, you ain't ever been into Boxing
You ain't into the locking, trapping, the grappling
But you're real good with the yapping
You should ask them, who'll have your back when cats start attacking
Ya know, when the real shit happens
They know there're cats out here stabbing and body bagging, duct tape gagging
Cats into kid-napping, that click clacking, gun clapping
Laughing matters last as long as the laughing matters
Until they got to gasp and gather the family after tragedy
Damn they were just laughing at you,
Some of them jokers you're joking with ain't joking
You ain't got your eyes nor your mind opened, they're into poking
You're just entertaining the folks who are pushing and promoting
They ain't your friends....

Your people will tell you when enough is enough,
Say to you "stop acting tough, before he calls your bluff,"
"Homie, you're fucking up"
"You've got a good thing, don't mess it up"
They'll keep it real with you
Your fan club will pump you up, but after Life comes to deal with you
The fan club would rather disappear then heal with you
You're a social media thug, don't let that plug get pulled
An internet celebrity, they've got you fooled
There are goons who'll take shit further than you're willing to go
Further than needed to be
You want them to pay attention, stop pretending before they're attending that
attention that comes for free
There are killers in these streets, your peeps love to hashtag and fake riots
They ain't your friends, if when it's time to speak up to save you, they're quiet
They ain't your friends....

Whenever you can look at all that together you've been through
And someone can say something and turn them against you
If your secrets aren't safe, loyalty misplaced, shrouded in jealousy and hate
When your name tastes of disgrace on their tongue
When you were in dire need to speak but your phone never rung
If you've spent nights alone bleeding, thinking about leaving
And people only come see you when they need you
They ain't your friends....

The Neutral…
Don't have your back when you are being attacked
Laughed at
But some will stand beside you,
then criticize you when you unleash the punch you pack
Cause you're wrong for that, their support you lack
At least an enemy will hurt you from the outside of your circle
Don't let their darkness usurp you
Most friends don't deserve you; they'll desert you
Some will last a season, some as long as a commercial
You'll never see their purpose on the surface
There are many kinds of serpents; look thru the mini blinds
Plenty times your curtains closed
When you were alone and the thoughts roamed
Who picked up the phone
If you were to go, who would have known your desires or your plans
You don't have any friends, you have fans
Stand-ins, users, abusers and posers, fakes, phonies, and snakes
They're not a part of your reality, they're just here for the show
They like to speak on, what they think they know
It's hard to decipher those with inner God – from those with underbelly scars
Those that slither usually wither away and decay anyway
They aren't meant to stay, they ain't built that way
They aren't made to last, that ass is to be taken out with the trash
They're trash, you may need to cut your grass
Some of those demons you'll support, even when being held back
Pitchforked tongues, run tell that
Loyalty, picture that
Most people are just searching for something to snicker at
They're lousy, their intentions cloudy
Clowns that move with crowds, they'll watch you drown
They'll hunt you down, they'll cut you down
Then smile when they come around
They don't know the hassles you battle with
Nor the baggage you travel with, how can they help you carry it
They just want to ride on your chariot when you're merry
Barely see the struggles you tussle with, they just wanna uncover it
Their relationship you coveted, once comforted
Too busy to pay attention, they've covered it and been discussing it
In the most disgusting manner, scammers and back stabbers
Stay in your company more often than not,
Sometimes they're all you've got
Stop relying on liars to be honest with you
"Honestly, I was with you." "I made a promise to you."

The irony is obvious, dig a grave to lay you in
There's only room for one
Lay your back to the dirt, you can still see the Sun
You can see them when they come, learn to leave them where they're from
Stop leaving them crumbs
Stop feeding the bums
They're leeches with tongues, speaking of your bleeding
When you're bleeding, when people you're in need of
They be speaking that "We need love" – but act like they've never seen love – it's foreign
They'd rather deface and shame you, when praising you gets boring
It's normal for 'em
They take off when the storm is forming
There are no neutral sides to take in war
You're either against or you're for, either the rich or the poor
Just because they're friends, don't mean that they're yours
They're just people looking for a ship to explore
Be careful for whom you open your door
When it's time to fill in the holes in your ceiling
You'll realize that real friends come one in a million

It's not that I don't believe in the scriptures
I just don't believe in the Scripters
I believe I was created in the image of
But I don't see Him in the pictures
This is why I ain't religious
Noble in how I'm living, I just ain't superstitious
I refuse to be taught the teachings by believers
Who hide the fictitious in their intentions

I wasn't there to see if the Pharisees would be fair to me
Every Saint I know is a sinner when compared to me
And it was my Soldiers, not the Church-goers who were there for me
I'm tithing to the charities 'til they bury me
I've fathered the Angels that carry me
I live by the real definition of G-code
Got God in my genome
With all this God I see in me, I believe to be
Any other deity forced upon me must be an imposter
They ain't got big enough guns for their weapons to prosper
But rape, hate and slavery, makes for one hell of a monster

Is Hell a concept or a construct
And how did we get false idols
When the devil prays to the same God that I do
And how am I to…. Believe in an Immaculate Conception
When 'Virgin,' just meant Mary and Joseph never had a wedding
I believe in blessings and learning from life's lessons
But I've seen too many churches tax you for your severance
Is this about finances or reverence
Which does it represent
How can the reprehensible be admissible
People think asking for forgiveness is the same as repentance
The difference is in if you meant it
The kinship, the friendship
Your innocence isn't contingent on their ability to sense it
Since God knows your heart
Since God wrote your part
When the sky is dark and the wind blows
God got your bark if you're rooted in Her

That's that, 'Faith the size of a Mustard Seed'
That's how the strength of our Mothers be
That's why I believe that God is a she
Cause she didn't whine when the water was cut off

73

Selling fishplates and bread to insure her children get fed
She gives blood, sweat and tears
And somehow hears the fears we've whispered
But the Bible says it's forbidden for women to minister
I don't believe at all – in Timothy or Paul
I believe the Serpent wrote some of these verses for the churches
And profits pushed Prophets to pull people from their purpose
Seems like, some Saints are only sanctified on the surface
Seems right, prayer without work is worthless
On my deen, I've seen the light, praying on my knees at night
It's my beliefs these demons fight
Ever since I stopped smoking on that Jesus pipe
I'd rather just call Him by His name His Momma gave him....

Trying to figure out who is lying, He lived a Jewish life and was crucified
How I live my life, I'll be damned if I let you decide
I believe in God
I believe in infinite wisdom and that sins can be forgiven
I don't believe in these systems
I don't believe every believer is a Christian
I don't believe in religion
Their truth is Holy cause there's holes in it
I look beyond the smoke and mirrors...
There's no business, like show business.

Sometimes love runs its course
Sometimes, love comes up short
Lovers held together by force, part in divorce
Sometimes you are so sure until it becomes war
Until you are drained of the love, sweat and tears you have poured
Keeping score of the scores, scars and scabs
How often the 'Goods' outweighed the 'Bads'
Still overlooking all of the 'goods' you used to have
Sometimes you clash, sometimes it's best to dash
It wasn't gonna last, you have to learn to sit back and laugh
Sometimes someone who once treated you like trash
They'll show their ass; they'll discard their half; bash you
Sometimes suck you dry - vacuum, cut up your clothes
Burn down your house
Neatly place your belongings on the curb, put you out
Bruise themselves, then claim you beat them
Sometimes, you will play that game too, but you won't defeat them
Sometimes, you thought you knew, but now you are about to meet them
Inner demons are the real them, you've been sleeping and creeping
With their representative
You think they are delicate and sensitive
Sometimes you realize, they are primitive
You hear the sayings, "Niggas is lazy," "Bitches are crazy"
Hypnotize yourself, "Don't let them phase me, Don't let them phase me."
"I won't let them change me."
Sometimes, some days you're all "I miss my Baby"
Going crazy, other times it's - what the fuck was I thinking
How'd this happen – that motherfucker snapping
Acting out of character
Sometimes, you find that they're that character and not an actor
Sometimes, we ignore the facts, deny the truth
Sometimes we're all Boaz and Ruth
Sometimes her broke ass is loose, she ain't speaking the truth
Too much masculinity made him aloof
Sometimes, we don't know when to shut up, sometimes you're both fucking up
Sometimes, we just don't mix
But that's no cause for her to act like a dick
Or for him to act like a bitch, stupid shit
People break up, separate, end their discussions
Breaking away from headaches shouldn't end in concussions
Sometimes you're mad, you've lost what you had
Sad cause you thought it was in the bag
Bit off more than you can chew, then you began to gag
Sometimes you're at fault, sometimes you're not, sometimes you share it

Grin and bear it, envy is an ugly shade of green, but sometimes we choose to wear it

Sometimes you got what you asked for, you were an asshole

Now handle it with class – hold your crown

Or drown in your misery

If it truly meant something to you, it should be "in loving memory"

Sometimes, we're just comfortable in our discomfort

Afraid to admit it, too stubborn to change it

Sometimes, life can be a bitch, but Love…

Love is a Motherfucker - Ain't it?

I'm tired…
Tired of screaming sirens and violence and blackened eyelids
Tired of fighting, I thought there was peace in silence
I'm tired of the silence – cold shoulders
Those passersby just passing by
I've heard my Daddy's lies, I've heard my mother cry
I've heard their disdain for such a burden as I –
"Life was simple before we birthed a cripple" she said
"I heard that!" he said
I heard what she said, then he said –
I should've been aborted, a mistake –
Then I heard her admit that I wasn't his, but the
Product of rape
I'm the part she hates
I hear every fight, every dispute
They don't know I'm not even deaf… I'm a mute
I've heard my soul bleed
They feed my needs but don't believe I can succeed
They've never heard me read; they don't believe I'll achieve
Just surrender, give up, concede
I've heard them say it
Like a broken record they play it daily
"Oh, hell, he can't hear us anyway," they say
They say, "I wish we could send him back, an accident"
How compassionate, my parents
Who've yet to realize that I'm drowning too deep into my depression
To make facial expression – they wouldn't hear me cry if I could
They don't look at me long enough to see these tears
They're the ones who can't seem to hear
They're the ones who don't seem to care that I'm right there
When they speak of me so harshly, they scare me
I've heard them curse my name; I've heard them express their shame
And complain –
Their words, torturing my heart, clawing at my mind
Momma, I have an inability to speak, my hearing is just fine
Daddy sometimes I just want to give you the finger for refusing to learn to sign…
Yet every time you've pantomimed, I've wished that I was blind
I hate seeing your face when you lie to mine
Reaching out to hug me like you love me, while spewing hate with your tongue
It's just like listening to you beat my mommy and saying
"I love you" when you're done – I heard that
Hating myself because I can't tell a soul, I can't scream!
But I can hear her heartbeat when she's scared…
Hear the pace racing, her trying to escape, wasting away

I can hear everything she has to say, before she takes it out on me
I've wished you both would've run out on me
I wished I was deaf, wished for death
I'm overwhelmed by the stress from y'all's mess
Since you thought I couldn't hear, you never told me about life's lessons
Or how to count blessings, never prayed with me…
Yet I've come to hear all the negative things you've had to say and they've
Stayed with me…
If I could speak – I'd at least, thank you for giving me life
But then again… I can write
Sincerely yours,
The Defective Child
That you can't seem to love right

SHE turns me on with everything about HER

She had…. Candles burning, I was yearning
My hands learning her curvature
While I was learning her, I serviced her
Thought she was deserving of better service
I held back from worship, cause I wanted to prey on her surface
Dig deeper beneath it until I laid on her cervix
She was perfect, but I was there for a purpose
Skin bare, I stared and could feel the surges, fought the urges
I licked my lips as my fingertips dripped with oils
I could feel the heat, my lust began to boil
Don't spoil the moment, it became too hard to hold it
I spoke, I broke the silence
Though I had already thought myself inside it, panties to the side
It was only wide enough for me… to see myself in it
I pretended to be comfortable, said, "Baby I'm here to comfort you"
But I was the one that needed comforting
Couldn't believe that my mind was wandering, wondering
If my tongue hit streams if she'd cream, if she'd scream
I was wide awake while I dreamed
My fingertips…. around her nipples and places that had dimples
She made faces when I traced the places that tickled
I know she was wet cause I could hear the ripples, the splashes
I kept seeing flashes, grabbing her ass and I spasmed
I shivered, I wanted her to want me to deliver
I wanted to make sure, I'd made her remember
Wrapped my hands around her tender figure
Built a bridge with her spine to claim her as mine
I wanted to suck my way from her toes to her mind
I was trying – it got hard to breathe, I was dying
It got hard to leave – I was a giant, swollen
I was holding back
My hands came face to face with her lap
Wanting to pry inside her hips and thighs
I let my fingertips glide, massaged
I was so beside myself that in my mind, she, me and I had already ménaged
I was tripping, it must've been written in the stars
I was kissing all her scars – but my lips never touched her…
That's when I knew how much I want her, but I want her
To trust me, she don't lust me any
Knowing if I had my way, she'd want me plenty, fuck me silly
These feelings weren't empty, there was more of a connection than my hands
connecting with her flesh
I was a mess, started to sweat, I mean I started to stress
I thought about sex, I thought about touching, I thought about fucking

I even thought about loving while I was rubbing her down
I wanted to drown in her cascades, but I had to behave
I thought I was brave until that wave hit and splashed
It wasn't planned that we'd sit and laugh
That when we crossed paths that we'd share our pasts
That we'd compare and contrast, or that our conversation would last
Until hours just passed, I was just past infatuated
Had masturbated in my mind several times
I had already climbed the walls, but in her eyes, I stood tall
But I had been weak since I had started massaging her feet
And thought about feasting and eating when our evening turned into midnight
And I was fighting to keep my lid tight
No lying, I was trying, I had the impatience of an In-patient dying
Hiding from temptation, hiding the fire with the temp raising, it was amazing...
My heart got to know her pain...
My hands got to show her pleasure...
My mind desired for her treasure as I survived through the pressure....
We got better acquainted as she lay naked
Heavenly, soft, sacred...
We shared a therapy session, but I still don't feel close enough to confront her....
I've traced her love with these fingertips to carry with me....
But damn, I still want her

Fellas, you ever had your ass ate…
I'm talking about when the tongue penetrates
And you don't know whether to escape or to punch her in her damn face
I mean… did it damn near make your stomach ache
It was all good when she was just giving you head and you were giving her face
You ever feel like she violated your personal space
I mean, you're trying to fight it, cause you don't know if you're supposed to like it
You would've never tried it willingly
But now your booty hole is tingling…. No pun intended
See personally my ass is an exit, not an entrance
There were no visits intended
I don't like feeling…. Defenseless
Does your heart plummet when she tells you to turn on your stomach
Do you get nervous when she's massaging your lower back and wind blows
across your crack
Do you cuff the sack…. Between your thighs when she touches your behind
Did you cry…. On the inside when her tongue was on the inside
Did your manhood flee, did you buckle at the knees
Does everything tighten up when she swipes your butt
Shut down…. When she comes around your brown round
Ever have to fight with the fact that you love her….
But now you know she's a nasty mother fucker
Brothers…. Did your ferocious inner Lion purr like a kitten when she was in that
hidden forbidden
Did you find yourself…. Committing to not submitting
Did you fight the urge to look back and say, "What the fuck are you doing?"
Was your pride ruined for the moment, did you hold it…
The screams and shouts you wanted to let out or did you let it fester and sequester
Did what just happen even register
Did you want to believe that lubrication was a hallucination
Did she conveniently leave out the part of her being a sexual deviant
Did she first, lick the scrotum when you turned over to give you some composure
She tricked you, before she licked you
And then she had the nerve to pucker up to kiss you…
Did you… give her that, 'if I had feeling in my legs I would kick you, side eye
roll' when she was Frenching your 'No Fly Zone'
Did you not want to tell her that, she was such an asshole…
Again with the puns….
And when she was done with the tongue
Did she then try to make her fingers, friends with your buns
Doesn't wet ass feel like, you just had the runs….
Gentlemen, has your backside been victimized in the name of having your sex life
energized
Did you not give consent before being stripped of your dignity…

Did some crazy hellion do to you what some sick vixen did to me…
If so…
There's help
But first you have to admit to self
Just how good it felt

Ladies… are you starting to hate when he presents the same lame dick
The Dead and Stiff
Are you getting less and less pleasure as he provides inch after inch
Don't you want that Relay Dick, that hand over fist, stick-stick
That shit that makes you gag and spit
Because you want to, because you have to
Not because he asked you
You want the type of dick that has to come with a warning
Have you making grits and eggs in the morning
But lately his performance has been getting dormant, it's boring
Has your love making been reduced to adoring the porn
Does it no longer rain when it storms
If so…. We're here to help
If you're tired of the usual Bump and Grind and 69
Try the "Spanish Fly," a special order, south of the border a.k.a "Sesenta Y Nueve"
It's just like the 69, but ya'll are eating ass
But … if you don't have a taste for that, you can pass
On to the next class
You want something that'll change your world
Try the "Somalian Swirl"
With just a twist of his hips while his Twix is betwixt the lips of your hips
Using his dick to stir the mix, is sure to hit……. All the walls
Fellas, if you want to astound her
Try the "Peruvian Pussy Pounder," mount her
Place her legs over your shoulders, lean forward
Push down until you cover her ears with her ankles, she'll thank you
Now insert the bone and drive it home
Ladies when you're riding, reverse Cowgirl and putting in work, Twerk
Hit him with that Kegel squeeze
Fellas fight back with the stroke of death, give her that Lethal D
That, "This shit should be illegal" D
Better known as….. "The Immaculate Ejaculate"
This is when you're being all passionate, then give her your deepest thrusts
Until she feels you reaching through her guts
One hand gripping her butt, shaking while you do it, but you ain't about to nut
Or lay her on her side, hit her with the "Gorgeous Glide"
Lay behind, grab her stomach and punish it the way she wanted it
Guaranteed to leave her thinking about that, "Being a Mother shit"
Now…. The "Russian Crushin'" is for maximum busting
Fuck around as a 'Man Crush Monday' and become a Husband
You'll need strong legs for the thrusting
A modified doggy-style, a more perverted perversion of its original version for the ultimate submersion excursion

After the body purging,
put your leg up by her arm until she can feel the surging
Grab ahold of her arm and mane, pull back on the reins
This is usually the part when she starts screaming your name, screaming she came
Talking in different dialects and languages
This move will have her showing up to your job at lunchtime with the sandwiches
This sexual position is the key to submission
And if you need to switch it up for a change, don't be ashamed
You want to show love the butt love, try the "Bulgarian Butt Plug".
We have yet to have it patent pended
But it still cums…. Highly recommended
If in the bedroom, you need to Shake things up a bit
Here at S.H.I.F.T……we got the Gift.

-Shift is not responsible for the production of stalkers, unplanned pregnancies, neck and back pain, sugar-daddies or turning your sleeping neighbors into enemies….
Order now for our 69-page manual with Endless Possibilities

All this rain just means she's still cumming from the last time we were touching
Her body covered in sweat from intense loving
Running up walls...
When her nature called
I came and made her Niagara fall
Choking from penetration
She spoke a forbidden language
Exchanging of making faces, amazing sensations
She came every time I tamed her waves
Every time I said her name, she rained
My tongue paved ways from navel to garden
My flesh hardened as the sound of our love began to sharpen
Closed our eyes, our skies darkened
Echoed the soft tone of her moans as we lost control
Her grip and hold kept me swollen
Our love continued to shape and mold as her hips rolled
As my lips kissed every fold, exploring her unknowns
Spreading her legs, sucking her toes
We're so familiar, she needn't tell me where to go
We stopped, locked eyes, locked lips
Fingers clenched
Her legs braided with mine, we intertwined
Position number 9, she wanted me from behind
It was art the way her back arched
The way our laps sparked when they clapped apart
She had my heart in her hands, our promise on her lips
My hips submerged in her thighs, my thighs wrapped in her hips
Her heavens I lay betwixt
Position switched, pinned her wrists
Dipped my gift deeper
To meet her sweeter fluids
Taking her to school, had been teaching her movements
A perfect student, no room for improvement
No need for adjustment
She was lusting for my thrusting
I had been longing for her loving
We were both getting what we wanted
I was gripping on her stomach
With every rise and plummet
Her plushness I would punish
My hands locked in her locks as she begged me not to stop
Role reversal, she got on top and started rocking the rocket
She started popping the private while she held me inside it
Switching the rhythm, changing her technique

Her head had me gripping the bedsheets
Making my legs weak, delayed speech
.....We fell asleep...
Drained, not an ounce remaining
Awakening to this storm
Feels good to know she's still raining.

I've been to many a places, accomplished many feats...
I've rocked many of stages, blazed on many beats
But the Artist in me feels incomplete...
Cause the God that's in me never sleeps
The Beast, he got to eat, I got to feed him
The Man I was yesterday, gotta beat him
Gotta weed him out, 'til my grandkids' grandkids read about
I ain't done yet, we ain't having fun yet
I ain't come up enough to see Son set
This is for the battles I ain't won yet
Creating a path for my son's steps, my daughter's flight deck
My life is but a segue to the verses I ain't write yet
Thought I'd killed them all but there are demons I ain't fight yet
I used to be used to getting paid, now I write checks
Paid in respect – threatened by No Weapon...
While they're stacking bread, I'm counting blessings
I've learned valuable lessons from lesser
Hold on when the foundation strong
Still things you got to get in order, brick and mortar
I got holes to fill, so I know the feel
Been surrounded by those who pose as real, so I know the deal

Want better for my young and loved ones.....That Golden Seal.....
Started in the yard, reached that Holy-Field
I went hard on the Mic when it came to the fight
My name rings bells in hell, a former shell

Keep my ready aim on that steady gain come heavy rain
Learned how to levee pain when my peers were learning how to hurry cane....
I got a monster to unleash on Earth beneath my surface
He used to feast on every belief that I was worthless
When the churches beckoned me from the streets and serpents
He was the Berserker that murdered the enemies within me
Myself, I stand between crossed hairs, a target
I'm talking, knowing the truth can get me killed
I am sword and shield, know what to absorb and what to yield
To be the core and rebuild...
I got to get right with those closest to me in order to stay on top
Yet just as Jehovah (Jay Hova) got that title (Tidal), my waves will never stop....
Boats rock even when docked, apocalypse upon my lips
I spit verses and sermons, I'm serving
Purpose driven by purpose
Selling a truth to the merchants that they don't have to purchase
No God Complex, I'm just trying to perfect the Perfect, tell it like I heard it

Preach it the way my Teacher been teaching
Some thought I was reaching, but now I'm seasoned, now I am Beacon
Now I walk with purpose and speak of reason
Each and every piece is deadly
Silence is golden, but even that peace is deadly
I speak it heavy and keep my speeches ready
Be the embodiment, essence, the epitome, example
Raise above the flames and be the mantle, handle being the head
Got to get back, sit back with my brothers and break bread....
Before I'm dead...

No matter the feats...
If I'm not right with those closest to me
I am not whom I am supposed to be.

Hospital read "Kings" on the moniker
Clenched fist, looked like I was spitting on the monitors
Took the lil King home, to his throne, a little home in Saratoga
Streets were a warzone, He – destined to be a soldier
Vulgar as he got older, the Arts taught him composure
How to shoulder the boulders without smoking them
When the gunshots woke him, gun smoke was choking him
Holding him hostage
Dirty crackpipes – Jersey turnpike
Moved to Golden State barely old enough to guard the estate
Counting tape and costly mistakes
Friends dying over whips and chains – never picked that cotton
We were rough riders before - X - had them popping
Fought over ashes, wish we could have got him before they shot him
Another Dark Knight in Gotham
It's had to crack smiles over crack vials
Picked up a pen to avoid one
The noise could have destroyed
I wrote to silence the sirens
Wrote to silence the firing, the lack of hiring,
When the cost of living was heightening, rising
I wrote to quiet my brothers and sisters crying out
Hunger pains, sleep deprived
We survived on free lunch and bread lines
Skimming obituaries, I was 14 when I read mine
Side walk chalk on that hop scotch
Traces from that 'pop, pop'
We dreamt of castles in this sandbox
Pushers in the parks and every sandlot
Trying to progress in the projects I was just a prospect
Wasn't my time yet
Death called like I'm next, but sometimes a parent's addiction is your prime threat
Sometimes section 8 ain't paid the rent yet, no mic check
King Vitamin, Kaboom and adding sugar to cheerios
Canned milk for the cereal was a blessing
Peanut butter and ramen – meal stretching when stressing
Turned weapon possessions from protection to a means for collections
Keep your anklets, bracelets and necklace
We had to hunt for lunch, dinner and breakfast
Stolen cars, goons would stunt, sons were reckless
No wall standing without Rest in Peace murals
Candle lit vigils – Brick City, streets with serial killers
Children "getting high" another innocent dies
No innocent lives, since Jersey Drive corrupted young minds

Don't be special – systems in place to level us
Learn to grip the metal before you mettle with the Peddlers
Successful settlers
Broken promises equivalent to empty wishes
So ambitious, grow superstitious, "These streets would bury us"
Peers started lighting up that dope – stressing
I started writing, it was dope, even when I'm broke, I never broke
Lessons - how to cook coke, how to fire the burner
Quick learners, whole sentence earners gave us sermons
I stuck to the scriptures
Outside the box, I was boxing – no blemishes
Martial Arts kept me disciplined, stay busy
It stayed with me
My baby brother faith never left the hospital to play with me
Promised Momma that 'Edy Ah' would grow old and gray with me
Decay with me
Nini moved away, Sky would stay, but Sunshine
got taken away by the hands of an angry man – I wrote eulogies
when I grew used to losing – never grew used to using
accepted abuse from users – when trying to help them
Never used them, never dealt them
Found them, tried to drown them down the toilet, destroy it
College campus – got no answers
Only faced AIDS and cancer
I've been stranded
Everywhere that I have landed, tho
Ain't been lost yet
6 holes in my body, titanium in my spine
Learned to climb before I could walk
Must've learned to rhyme before I could talk
I've been places…
Since I've been gone from where I was born, lived long
Beyond being wronged or strong armed – this Man formed
In Pure Form
Eye see 3 dimensionally with Me, Myself
And I've always been there for 'em…
Insight eight moves ahead, always come prepared for 'em
I've seen sights, heard sounds, smelled decaying carcasses
This isn't life, its art and art is just…
Graffiti on the walls… where I come from
Let me speak of my journeys

Mothers in a manner in which
I could only dream to Father~

Your Highness….
I know you love your child like only a Mother can love
You feel and ache in your body, breath in your lungs
When something doesn't belong, you sense that it's wrong
Your connection strong
And you hold on with your grip when she's slipping away
Like rose petals, slip and wither away
You fear she'll stray, begin to decay and you didn't raise her that way
I know…. That I'm not the gardener you trust in your Flower's bed
That I may never meet your approval
But I'll prove you wrong on any account you doubt me about, don't count me out
Because of you, your daughter – perfectly made
And though I wasn't made perfectly, I was perfectly raised to fit her perfectly
Maybe today, undeservingly
But I beg of you time to prove
That I can make mountains move
Have her old scars removed and soothe her bruises
I am not the perfect package by any means
But that doesn't mean it isn't worth it
That we can't be perfect together
That forever won't come and go before we know it, that one another we can't
grow old with
I love your daughter…
I wish I could say that I knew the very 1st time I saw her
I wish I knew a love like this existed
Back when "Love" was just a fancy word for affection and sexual connection
Before I knew love had psychological, physical and spiritual effects on me
No… I love your daughter, I am constantly in awe
I adore her flaws and admire the picture she paints every time she moves her jaws
Her mind is brilliant
Like the Sun – In your world, she's your daughter
In mine she is the Sun
Her eyes tell stories of God's creation on the surface
But deeper I've seen the hurting, the backstabbers, the serpents
I've seen the good battle evil, blessings battle curses
I listen to the joy in her voice and the pain written in her verses
I pay attention – to the rise and fall of the arches in her sole's when she walks
I'm trying to grab ahold of her soul when we talk
Her body is not a property on which I wish to embark
She is not a territory on which I'll leave a mark
She's a god that you've blessed with a body and heart
And I'm not trying to part her seas, plant my seeds and leave
To me she is life, air and oxygen – and I'm trying to breathe….
Good intentions, bad position

I am no mathematician, but my addition will be greater than our division
I've listened to her heartbeat and only heard the Angels rejoicing
Maybe I'm crazy, but only your baby has quieted the voices
I know life is about choices, sometimes we live with regret
We tend to fret and stress before we realize we're blessed
I've found a happiness…. That I was never even looking for
A religion, that I've never believed in
And I know attempting to compare my love for her to yours
Would be an armless man reaching, but honestly speaking
What I believe is….
She is my heaven, she is my beacon…
She is my every day, and I the knight sent to slay her demons….
I will love her, protect her with my life until the day I die
My only regret was not receiving your blessing first, but I'll ask again and
again….
"Mother May I…?"

Duck and cover
Find you one brother you will roll with
Consider that friendship a Gift
Cause many befriend a pretender, know when to cut them off
When to dismember a member and remember
You'll be judged on race, religion and gender
Learn when to let go and when to pull the trigger
Be bigger than your enemies, they will outnumber you
You, continue to shine through the darkness, the same way the Thunder do
Be better than your Father, Be the Man I wanted to
They will hunt for you, they will come for you
You give them your Mother's attitude and your Father's spine
No hell or high water will drown a child of mine
Don't follow in no Footsteps, make your own
I may fail building you an Empire, you got to take your throne
Know this, you will be born more man than most of my peers
You'll find strength in your mother's tears
Educate yourself, understand that wisdom comes with years
Believe what it is you see, question everything you hear
Remove fear from your heart – Remember if it wasn't for the dark
You'd never notice the stars
If you're too afraid to get naked, they'll never notice your scars
Junior you got to go hard; I mean you're gonna have to bowguard
You're going to have to know God – He looks just like you
Find that light inside you – Shine Baby, they already fear you
Their mantra, "Melanin Makes Monsters of Men"
Dark skin ain't sin
Move mountains my Son… Run Boy Run
Hit every finish line, quitting time ain't in our language
I may be unable to explain it, but just being you is dangerous
You were born to raise a nation
Treat your sisters like the Gods they are, protect them
Respect them, ensure children never know neglection
Touch the woman you love with your Energy, not your Erection
Love her like God so loved the world, like I love your Mother
Know the difference between time to give your life and time to duck – and cover
There's a Warrior in your Bloodline, History in your Helix strands
The Genius in your Genome, won't keep the blood off your hands
You got to keep your blade sharper, hit harder, be smarter than your Father
You've got to go farther, be a better Father than your Father
You've got a Father that'll die for you, so that you may live for yours
Junior don't you fight to live, you give them Wars
Never be ashamed of who you are – African, West Indian, Creole
Your Father's first thorn, your Mother's first born – God

Know that when I'm gone, when you lay to rest my flesh
That I am with you – every step, through every breath
I have loved you since you were a thought and conversation
Discussion, contemplations and ovulations – I don't believe in miracles…
I believe in you…
I wanted to leave this world better than how I found it
And I am proud… leaving it you.
They may be undeserving, callused when you meet them
Some may not understand who you are my Son… Teach Them

Momma Said

Momma said, "My Son....
My Son, if you don't see many a profit then drop it
Either be Prophet or receive many a Doctorate
Stray away from white sheets and Police dockets
Any thought of you being less than, stop it
And always keep a promise; You promise?"
I said, "I Do," she said, "When you tell her that, mean it
No one come in between it, make a mess - you clean it
Cultivate it before you leave it, say it – mean it
Deem it necessary then be 'It,' Legendary – My Son....
When you run, run the world.... Wherever you go"

My Momma taught me most of what I know
Hell No, I ain't ready for her to go – she mine
I didn't learn how to cry until she began fighting to survive
Like when I was 6 and he was 9, momma crept up from behind and screamed
"Hawk, you better whoop that boy's behind"
Or grade 4, when them 4 jumped her son and she walked them down
One by one for us to shoot 'fair ones'
And when 8 teens on South 18th had beef
With me she stood, back to back and fought back
She fought, scraped, Momma fought crack
Yeah, she fought that
Bought snacks when she could only afford scraps – made meals
And no matter how bad we'd feel, she made us heal in a way that gave us chills
She said, "My Son, My Son …Nation Build
When Nay say – build!"
Ak, I've watched my mom fight with Cops who had me in their possession
She ran up – no weapon, willing to die for my protection

And though the life she's lived has made her crazy
I ain't ever NOT been my Momma's Baby
You can't imagine the power, the passion, the pain that she gave me
Pop may have trained me, but I know my Momma made me
I so wanted for God to take me instead, but Momma said,
"Pooh, you've got shit to do....
You've got **M**ountains to **M**ove, **M**onsters to **C**onquer, **C**ancers to **C**ure
My young **E**m**c**ee, you've got a way with words and you'll always win
You are the most wonderful, warrior I've ever witnessed"
That Woman wise…She wrote poems with her womb
The Creator only created one woman like *Ennis*
She left me her wish-list, so before my lifetime has ended
Everything on her hitlist, I will have finished
Momma said, Momma said, "When you earn it, let no one take it
They will strip you naked, knock you down then lock you up for being vagrant

If you can't find it – create it
Ain't no flag waving, we don't give 'ups nor fucks'
Be persistent in your purpose, poised in your position
Never be distracted by the noise of opposition
You don't need competition nor confirmation
You, My Son are conqueror of nations, King of Kings, Lord of Lords"
She said, "I was told by my Father, that my Son's tongue would be sharper than
any sword"

My Mother…. Told me, that in every truth I utter, every script I scribe
She will be alive long after she's died
The farther I climb, the higher I rise
The closer I'll come to closure, so to keep composure
I'll keep composing, just knowing she was chosen
Momma said, "6 million ways to die, and still they ain't figured me out
My Son…. How can you have doubts?"
And just like my Mother, I've been beaten down, but not out
Just like she would tell me – Life, it doesn't play fair
But we either roll with the punches or get the hell out of the game
Now, I don't complain, I sustain, I maintain, I claim….
All that is mine, and all of it's mine
My Mother, is mine…and life tries to pry away what is mine
They say, "Death, you can't deny," but he's failed every time
Yet every time I smell an end getting near, see a future unclear
Or imagine her voice being the voice – I can no longer hear, I grow scared
It is all that I fear
Momma said, "My Son, I will always be here"
And that is all…. I ever needed to hear

DEDICATED TO:

My Mother,
My Lover,
My Lover's Mother,
My Sisters,
My Daughters,
and most importantly.........................to HER!

Shake is an accomplished Spoken Word Artist, published author and Slam Poet. He is also a two-time National Team Slam finalist and facilitates writing workshops for adults and children. *The Book of Her* is his 3rd book. Shake is still currently performing live at local venues around central Texas area.

www.shakemadness.com

**Also available from
Richard White
on
Amazon
and
310brownstreet.com**

www.ingramcontent.com/pod-product-compliance
Lightning Source LLC
La Vergne TN
LVHW091227080426
835509LV00009B/1195